Reading Cicero

Duckworth Classical Essays
Series editor: Thomas Harrison

Ancient Democracy and Modern Ideology

P.J. Rhodes

Interpreting Classical Texts

Malcolm Heath

Reading Cicero

Catherine Steel

DUCKWORTH CLASSICAL ESSAYS

Reading Cicero

Catherine Steel

Duckworth

First published in 2005 by
Gerald Duckworth & Co. Ltd.
90-93 Cowcross Street, London EC1M 6BF
Tel: 020 7490 7300
Fax: 020 7490 0080
inquiries@duckworth-publishers.co.uk
www.ducknet.co.uk

© 2005 by Catherine Steel

All rights reserved. No part of this publication
may be reproduced, stored in a retrieval system, or
transmitted, in any form or by any means, electronic,
mechanical, photocopying, recording or otherwise,
without the prior permission of the publisher.

A catalogue record for this book is available
from the British Library

ISBN 0 7156 3279 5

Typeset by Ray Davies
Printed and bound in Great Britain by
CPI Bath Ltd

Contents

Introduction

'When a commentator, a literary scholar, and a student of philosophy pick up Cicero's *On the state*, they each pay attention to different things.'[1] Seneca's multiplicity of approaches is still the rule in Ciceronian studies, though we can add to his trio those concerned with his biography, with late Republican politics, with Roman intellectual history and with the development of oratory. The variety of methodological approaches is a tribute to the extraordinary nature of Cicero's achievements as a writer of speeches, letters, poetry and treatises. Given the volume of his writing, in specialised studies it is also a necessity. But splitting his oeuvre and his activities can obscure as well as enlighten.

This book puts Cicero the writer and Cicero the politician together through an exploration of how he uses written texts to exist and operate within the public sphere. In turn the public dimension is always present when reading Cicero. The point is not simply that Cicero's writings must be sited in their historical contexts in order fully to be understood; it is only by dealing with all of his works as a single oeuvre that we can understand the extent of Cicero's achievement in turning writing into a tool which the politician at Rome could use to advance his career. I argue that he uses a multiplicity of genres in order to multiply the opportunities to tell his story; and innovates within the generic possibilities initially available precisely in order to tailor what he could write to who he was. A fundamental error is to assume that his philosophy and poetry are not 'political'; Cicero's writings could not escape from the public figure, and the issue is rather to consider the nature of the interaction between his various personas and writings.

A brief summary of Cicero's life is thus appropriate.[2] He was born in 106 BC at Arpinum, a town some sixty miles east and south of Rome. Its citizens had received the Roman citizenship in 188, and one of them, Marius, made a powerful impact on Rome shortly after the time of Cicero's birth; but the Tullii Cicerones, although prominent in Arpinum and related through marriage to Marius' family, had not yet become involved in Roman politics. Cicero, however, and his younger brother Quintus, were taken as adolescents to Rome to receive further education; and Cicero served during the Social war, which broke out in 91 BC between Rome and its Italian allies. During the 80s he studied rhetoric and then philosophy; he gave his first speech, in a civil case, in 81 and probably acquired brief notoriety the following year by acting as sole defence advocate in a high profile murder case. He then continued his studies in the Greek east before returning to Rome and embarking on a political career: he managed to win election to each in the sequence of magistracies 'in his year', that is at the earliest point permitted, becoming consul in 63 BC.

It was at this point that a career remarkable only for its ease, given Cicero's status as a 'new man', took a turn with wider ramifications. Towards the end of 63 Lucius Sergius Catilina, a member of the Senate who was already suspected of plotting to seize power, raised an army in Etruria. Cicero's colleague Gaius Antonius took charge of the military operations, but Cicero himself arrested a number of Catilina's accomplices in Rome and had five of them executed. The Senate supported the executions, but the legality of the action was highly questionable, since none of the men had been tried. Initially Cicero withstood criticism, but in 58 he was forced into exile by one of the tribunes of the year, Publius Clodius. He was recalled the following year and attempted to rebuild his authority; in 51 he was sent as governor to Cilicia and by the time he returned to Rome, at the end of 50, the civil war between Pompeius and Caesar was on the point of breaking out. Cicero sided reluctantly with Pompeius, whose supporter and ally he had intermittently been for nearly two decades. After Caesar's victory he was eventually allowed to return to Rome, where he took some part in public life as well as writing extensively on philosophy. When Caesar was assassinated he hesitated about taking a stand against Marcus Antonius, who had moved rapidly to assume Caesar's position, but in September 44 he delivered the first of the fourteen speeches orchestrating the senatorial opposition, which he called the *Philippics*. In the summer of 43, however, Marcus Antonius joined forces with two other important military figures, Marcus Lepidus and Octavian (Caesar's great-nephew, and heir) and thereby took control of Rome; Cicero was killed in the proscriptions which followed. He was married twice: first, in the early 70s, to Terentia, whom he divorced in 47 or 46; secondly, at the end of 46, to his ward Publilia, who was over forty years his junior, a marriage which lasted only a few weeks. He and Terentia had two children, a daughter Tullia, born fairly soon after the marriage, who died in childbirth in 45; and a son Marcus, born in 65, who survived the civil wars and proscriptions and was consul in 30; he is not known to have had any descendants.

Cicero was by no means the first member of the Roman elite to engage in literary activity; indeed, the authorship of many kinds of writing was restricted to this group.[3] Writing initially became an activity of public figures because oratory was one of their tasks, and writing allowed the preservation of speeches and their dissemination to a wider audience: an extension, that is, of a speech in both time and space. Orators had been producing written versions of their speeches since the middle-second century; the elder Cato is the most prolific, though not the earliest example. Historiography by Romans begins even earlier, with Fabius Pictor's history in Greek written towards the end of the third century BC; the first historiography in Latin was the elder Cato's *Origines*. The technical prose treatise developed rather later: the first legal work is Brutus' dialogues on civil law from the end of the second century.[4] At about the same time Marcus Antonius produced his small book on rhetoric, and Scaurus his memoirs; Sulla's memoirs, in twenty-two volumes, mark a further development in scale and ambition.[5] What these productions share is not only senatorial authorship but also an intimate relationship with the public activities of these men. The speeches of which written versions were disseminated were those delivered in the course of public activity, be it contributions to senatorial debates, to civil proceedings, or to criminal trials. Legal writing can be seen as an extension of the jurisconsult's traditional function of producing authoritative spoken responses to queries. Political memoirs can by definition be written only by those who have personal experience; and the Romans readily adopted the Thucydidean model of historiography which regarded it as the fit activity for the retired statesman, where experience of political and military affairs was an essential prerequisite for their analysis in written format. In contrast, though epic and drama were early transferred into Latin, their authors remained for the most part of relatively low status and the act of writing an opportunity for elite patronage rather than elite production. The group of aristocrats who wrote erotic verse towards the end of the second century were amusing themselves with a trivial art-form; with the exception of Lucilius' *Satires*, prose was still the medium for serious writing among the elite.

However, although there was, by the time that Cicero entered public life, this fairly substantial body of prose works by members of elite which reflected and preserved aspects of their public activity, it was by no means the case that the transition to written form was an automatic process. Most speeches perished at the moment of utterance; most forensic activity went unrecorded. And in the field of oratory it is clear that many of the most distinguished practitioners, particularly in the generation immediately before Cicero's, simply decided that they would not preserve their speeches in written form. Cicero had precedents for his decision to write, but it remained a choice.

What, then, were the mechanics of producing written texts? How did these texts reach their readers, and who were the readers?[6]

Essentially, a text entered the public domain as soon as its author had a copy made and gave it to someone else, or allowed someone else to copy his original version. The term publication, with its implications of the dissemination of multiple and identical copies, of the mediation of the relationship between writer and reader through a variety of intermediaries such as the publisher and the bookseller, and of a commercial motive underlying the process, is thus highly misleading. The dissemination of Cicero's texts was initially a deeply personal process: he passed on his work, whether in a copy he had had made, or in the original or a copy thereof destined for copying and return, to those he hoped might read it. And once he had allowed any copy into someone else's hands he had lost control of it. He would be unable to prevent the person who now had a copy from passing it on to his or her friends, for them to read and copy as they chose. There were no laws of copyright in Rome. Allowing a text to enter someone else's hands was thus irrevocable.

Nor did the process bring any immediate commercial gain. This was not simply because a writer had no recourse against others making copies of his work if they could get hold of it; there is no evidence that anybody paid to receive the initial copies from the author. If anything, having texts disseminated would involve the writer in expenses himself, if he was preparing copies of his work to give to other people. Insofar as there was a commercially viable book-trade at Rome, it was those who produced the physical items – the copies of texts – who made money. On the other hand, it is important not to overestimate the expense of producing texts. It is true that they required laborious copying by hand. But for someone who possessed a copyist among his slaves, the labour would not be a cost if the slave was not thereby distracted from other work: the outlay would only be in papyrus and ink.

Thus there is a paradox. Texts spread initially in a way that was highly personal: the author passed them on to personal acquaintances whom he hoped would read them. Thereafter, the process was, at least potentially, unknowable and the writer might have no idea who had read his work and who possessed a copy, or in what form his work was circulating. Even when he could track its progress and reception through networks of acquaintances, there could never be a guarantee that he knew of all the copies in existence, or of all the variations which might have crept into his text. Hence the possibilities for enormous fluidity in authorship, and a tendency for writings to be wrongly ascribed to famous writers.

This picture of a process of dissemination that was highly personal in the first stages does not, however, imply that Cicero left the circulation of his writings to chance. In the later part of his life we know that he relied heavily on Atticus and his trained band of copyists to produce multiple copies of his work. Nor need we believe that Cicero planned less carefully earlier in his career. The act of allowing written works to circulate under his name was always a considered one.

Why did Cicero disseminate written texts? As already indicated, the central contention of this book is that an element in his motivation was always some concern for the nature of his public profile. Nor is this a motivation true only of Cicero: rather, any politically active member of the elite, who also wrote, could expect those who read his works to do so with a consciousness of his public profile. Even works which set themselves up as irrelevant to public life, or as frivolous, or trivial, could not be divorced from political significance, given the loaded cultural significances both of dealing with Greek culture and of how one spent one's leisure time.[7]

The question, then, in reading Cicero is not simply what the political relevance is of a particular speech, or poem, or treatise. It should also be why Cicero chose to write down and disseminate that particular work. Hence the importance of 'reading': not simply an acknowledgement that our own engagement with Cicero is, unavoidably, dependent on written texts, nor even a reminder of the limits which uncertainty about delivery and gesture impose on our understanding of ancient rhetoric. It is also a response to the fact that Cicero chose to create for himself a textual presence. He first entered public life as an orator; his reputation, and success, were intimately bound up with his capacity to speak persuasively. To supplement those achievements with a permanent written record of what was said was to enter a different arena and one which many of Cicero's most distinguished predecessors as orators had not; this was a move which involved new audiences, new opportunities for criticism and the creation, conscious or not, of a record of who and what Cicero had been over the course of many years. And Cicero supplemented oratory with poetry and with rhetorical and philosophical treatises: in both cases he developed a new kind of writing, and new capacities for being a public figure in written form.

Cicero's initial readers were thus participating in his extension of political life at Rome from the geographically limited, time-specific and predominantly oral round of legislation and elections to a lasting and variegated record of an individual's contribution to public affairs. Our experience as readers of Cicero must also be grounded

12

in a sense of this transition towards permanent memorialisation. But in important respects our reading differs from that of his contemporaries. It is limited, inasmuch as our access to the underlying political arena is solely through written texts, even though Cicero's own evidence can and must be supplemented by other sources; and it is limited too by a necessarily imperfect grasp of Cicero's language and by the incomplete preservation of his output. But our experience of reading also permits a scope not necessarily available to Cicero's contemporaries. Above all, we are in a position to survey the surviving corpus as a unity: an experience denied to his first readers through the chronological extent of Cicero's writing career over a period of nearly fifty years, and, in all likelihood, constrained for most readers by the vagaries of access to copies. This synoptic view can assist us as readers in transcending Cicero's short-term aims and in seeking rather to perceive the larger trends which structure his writings and, at times, undermine Cicero's own grand narrative.

Cicero's use of writings as an element in being a public figure can also be seen as a response to the problems involved in such an occupation. The concept itself is elusive. There is no single word with which to translate 'politician' into Latin; and, as I discuss in Chapter 2, how to define what it means to be engaged in politics at Rome is a recurrent preoccupation in the three great treatises of the late 50s, *On the orator*, *On the state* and *On the laws*. The issue was one that lay at the heart of the Roman political system, since a form of government in which those who have power, that is the magistrates, hold office for a year and a year only, and cannot proceed from one magistracy directly to another, inevitably means that those who have held high office, and who will hold high office in the immediate future, will spend substantial periods out of office. Even those who reached the consulship might actually be magistrates for only four, or even three, years out of period of possibly fifty years or more, taking as a starting point for the measurement their tenure of the most junior magistracy, the quaestorship, which conferred senatorial membership, which could be held at the age of thirty. And the majority of the Senate never proceeded beyond the quaestorship, particularly in the period after Sulla: these are men whose tenure of public office might occupy only a year. Of course there was a wide variety of positions apart from the regular progression of the *cursus honorum* which could occupy senators: embassies, legal commissions, military positions, and a variety of official and less official positions within the staff of provincial governors. But the problem remained: even the most eminent would spend most of their time divorced from executive power. Hence the importance of the concept of *auctoritas*, translated as 'standing' or 'influence', as a means to express the idea that individuals could continue to affect events even when they were not holding office.[8] But during Cicero's adult life the problem, always present in the nature of Roman political life, gained an extra dimension as the phenomenon of the extended military command offered, to a small number of men in public life, the opportunity to avoid extended periods of leisure. Pompeius held *imperium* for twenty-nine of the thirty-five years between 83 and 48 BC and Caesar's *imperium* was unbroken from 59 until his death in 44; and though no one else matched the record of either of these men in length of service there were other examples of extended commands, including Crassus' five-year command in Syria, curtailed by his death, and Gabinius' and Piso's five-year commands after their consulships in 58.

The extended military commands posed a particular challenge to a man such as Cicero, whose public life, most unusually, did not include much military experience or achievement. These extended commands were of course the glittering prizes of the late Republic, attained by a tiny minority: most of those who reached the praetorship and consulship still held their subsequent military commands on the basis of the well-established pattern of annual prorogation by the Senate, even if pressures on manpower meant that actual periods in office increasingly extended to two or three years. But Cicero had removed himself from even this possibility, declining to take a province after his praetorship, and publicly renouncing his consular province in 63. How, then, could he maintain his position in public life in the intervals between office-holding, and even more so once he had attained the consulship – assuming, that is, that he wished so to do? As events turned out, the aftermath of the execution of the Catilinarian conspirators meant that retirement was not a possibility. In practical terms, Cicero's response both before and after his exile was to spread his account of events in as many different genres as possible; but in the late 50s he also turned to exploring the nature of continuing civil power within the state, encapsulated in that most misunderstood figure of the *rector rei publicae.*

Indeed, there are clear chronological patterns in Cicero's different genres. The speeches belong to two periods, 81-52 and 46-43; each has a distinct profile, the former containing a preponderance of forensic speeches with a number of deliberative speeches after 66, the latter the three Caesarian speeches and the fourteen *Philippics.* The treatises, with the exception of the early *On invention,* all date from the last twelve years of Cicero's life, that is 55-43; and here too there is a clear division, between those written before the outbreak of civil war in 49, that is the trilogy of *On the orator, On the state* and *On the laws,* which all arise directly from Cicero's experience in public life and his perception of the nature of Rome; and the series of works begun during Caesar's dictatorship (and spilling over into the months after Caesar's assassination) which tackle the whole of philosophy as it had been defined by that point. Cicero's poetry can be divided into early works, heavily influenced by Hellenistic poetry, and two attempts, in the period after his consulship (*His Consulship* and *On his Vicissitudes*) to use hexameter epic in order to write political autobiography. And finally there are his letters, which survive only from 66 onwards, are relatively patchy up until the civil war, and exist in huge quantities from 49 BC until a year or so before Cicero's death. Thus we have access to Cicero in different ways at different points in his career: as a young man we perceive him as a writer on rhetoric and as a poet; when a rising politician, as an orator; in his political ascendancy, as an orator, epic poet and intermittent letter writer; and in the decade from 55 onwards, as a philosopher, intimate correspondent, and flatterer of Caesar; and finally, as the defender of freedom. The extent to which the shifting forms of Cicero's writings have affected how subsequent ages have interpreted his life is a question too large in scope for this study, but one worth consideration as one reads biographies of the great man.

In addition to the chronological variation there are also difference in means of dissemination. Most important of these differences is the status of Cicero's correspondence. His letters were not disseminated in collected form during his lifetime: each letter was directed at a single reader, as opposed to Cicero's other works where a wide audience was sought and where Cicero could not control the ultimate range of readers. One can ask, therefore, what part the letters can legitimately have in a study of the ways in which Cicero creates his public persona. I discuss this issue in detail in Chapter 1; my conclusion, in summary, is that while the letters to Atticus are usually intended for him alone (though this privacy cannot be guaranteed) many of the other letters presuppose a wider audience than the recipient alone, or are in themselves manifestations of Cicero's public persona due to the identity of the person to whom he is writing.

Generic distinctions between Cicero's writings are themselves problematic. It is possible to divide all of his works into four groups: letters, speeches, treatises and poetry. But each division can be challenged. The surviving treatises include both philosophical and rhetorical works: it is not clear that these two categories belong most closely together, and the feeling that 'treatises' is a cover-all term to encompass those of Cicero's works which do not fit in elsewhere grows when one considers that the category also includes the lost accounts of his consulship and posthumous defence of the younger Cato. Cicero's poetry also contains at least two distinct types of writing, his early poetry, seemingly closely derived from Hellenistic models when not actual translations, and his hexameter works written as a senior politician. Even the speeches, written within the most clearly articulated of genres, include such experimental works as *On behalf of Marcellus*. And one could posit other categories which cut across these generic divisions: the most obvious would be translations, since Cicero translated poetry, philosophy and oratory from the Greek.

Nonetheless these divisions do offer a starting-point for a survey of what Cicero wrote, how we might want to categorise it, and how it fits in with contemporary Latin literature, which is the subject of Chapter 1. I stress that his achievement as an innovator extends far beyond his oratory, and that we should see him as a decisive figure also in the creation of the philosophical dialogue in Latin and in the reception of Hellenistic poetry at Rome. Indeed, oratory is one of

16

the areas where Cicero appears to innovate least. But the point of the exercise is not simply to set Cicero up as cultural hero, or to illustrate Caesar's assessment of him as a man who pushed back the boundaries of the Roman intellect.[9] What emerges most strikingly is Cicero's disregard for genre. In his history of oratory, *Brutus*, his anxieties about his work arise not from his rivals, but from the overwhelming consciousness that political change has rendered his skills unnecessary. His poetry and philosophica can contain, or even be, translations without any apparent concern for the integrity of his own voice. It is not that there are no generic rules at all, though studies of his oratory, by far the most formalised kind of writing he employed, have shown how flexibly he handled rhetoric and how its guidelines were subordinate to the demands of a particular case. The most reliable thing about Cicero's writing is ultimately his style, and in that, at least towards the end of his life, he seems to have been distinctly aberrant. But even in relation to the so-called 'Atticist/Asianist controversy' a reading of Cicero without preconceptions can yield the impression that scholarship has created a systematic stylistic debate in place of a brief spat. Cicero's approach to genre is a matter of seeing opportunities for multiplying his output; his oratory could be supplemented, or replaced if the climate demands, by his poetry and by prose writing other than oratory.

The potential of a lot of different kinds of writing is most easily traced in relation to Cicero's handling of the Catilinarian conspiracy. His actions as consul dominate the subsequent remaining twenty years of his life; and his presentation of his consulship forms the centre of the next chapter on Cicero as a public figure. Almost as soon as the conspirators had been executed it became clear that Cicero would face intense, and potentially destructive, criticism of his actions. His response was to disseminate, in an extraordinarily varied range of forms, justifications of his actions. Using different genres thus enabled Cicero to repeat his message, offering a variety of perspectives on a single vision, that is of Cicero as the saviour of the Roman state. But after his return from exile – exile which was a direct consequence of the execution of five of the Catilinarian conspirators – his self-presentation changes. He stresses his membership of a wider community rather than his individual heroic actions:

a response to the realities of a political environment in which Cicero's hopes for his position had not been realised, but one which transmutes weakness into a positive regard for the values of senatorial government. His textual presences are thus always in negotiation with the way that they are received; audience assent is essential if his writing is to succeed.

Cicero's modification of his consular persona leads into a more general consideration of the communities he acknowledges in his writings. His forensic speeches provide opportunities to place himself in regard both to his clients and to other advocates; and despite the antagonistic nature of the encounter the written versions of speeches frequently record amiable dealings with speakers on the opposite side. In his letters of recommendation we can see existing relationships being evoked to secure specific and concrete ends; the letters to exiles, by contrast, demand passivity and justify Cicero's acquiescence in the Caesarian regime. His treatises, too, show his range of connections through their dedications; but they also articulate imagined groups as Cicero creates communities of great Romans to which he too belongs. The communities evoked in the treatises can also be read as a prolonged lament for the transformation in Roman political life brought about by the civil war and Caesar's dictatorship.

In the final chapter I develop this exploration of failure and loss. Failure was always part of the Roman political system because of its competitive nature, and oratory marked the points at which failure was a possibility; but Cicero was, unsurprisingly, reluctant at most times during his career to record failures. The one major exception, his speech *On behalf of Milo*, is in fact the least bad option in the circumstances: although Cicero's client had been convicted, the existence of an unauthorised version of what Cicero had said at the trial meant that Cicero needed to respond with his own account. But in the Caesarian period failure becomes not an awkward fact to be concealed where possible but the defining aspect of public life. Cicero foregrounds his exclusion from politics in the prefaces to his treatises; and his two major works on oratory from this period, *Brutus* and *Orator*, both act out the consequences of this exclusion because they show that it is only possible to engage with speaking from historical or technical perspectives: there is no longer a performance presence.

Chapter 4 concludes with the *Philippics*, a set of speeches which have a heroic part in the narrative of Cicero's life, given their connection with his death; but these are also writings which constantly exploit Cicero's textual presence as a public figure, supplanting his concrete physical manifestations as part of an attempt to orchestrate the magistrates of the Roman Republic over an enormously extended area, and a period of months, in the struggle against Marcus Antonius. As such they mark the culmination of Cicero's articulation of himself as a textual presence, as well as a consular pursuing a particular policy.

Cicero was engaged in a transformation of the textual possibilities available to him in order to pursue his ambitions in the public sphere. That is, in addition to the forms of writing which were already established, and which arose directly from the activities of the elite, he created new forms of writing which did not. This expansion not only enabled him to express himself in a variety of ways, and thus tell his story over and over again, but also to circumvent the limits that his actual public career imposed. Written oratory was dependent upon spoken oratory: the connection could be avoided on occasion, but surely not completely ignored. But poetry and treatises gave Cicero the opportunity to write and disseminate a public persona even when he was not participating directly in public debates. They provided a means of extending himself outside Rome and of transcending the restrictions to which his career was periodically subject.

Cicero's writings are an enormous corpus, and this is a short book: inevitably I have been selective. There is less about the speeches, particularly from the period before his consulship, than might be expected: but Cicero's oratory has been the subject of a great deal of work in recent years, and the speeches are the least difficult part of his writings from the perspective of using texts to exist within the public sphere.[10] I have tried to take the poetry seriously: certainly I have not wished to follow Douglas who, in one of the few studies of Cicero's writings to attempt a view of the entire oeuvre, wrote: 'I have followed … my own inclination in saying nothing of the verse'.[11] And there is little on the philosophical

19

content of the philosophical treatises, and no attempt to assess his contribution to, or relationship with, the Hellenistic schools. I have concentrated instead on the ways in which Cicero himself describes his achievement, and on how he puts the activity of doing philosophy into a Roman context. But I have also tried to give adequate space to the close reading of selected passages: Cicero's writing is subtle as well as voluminous, and close attention to detail must be the basis of any broader interpretations.

Translations are my own; references to sources follow the system used in the *OLD*.

It remains to thank those whose support has helped me to write this book. I am grateful to the University of Glasgow for a term's leave and to the Arts and Humanities Research Board for an award under their research leave scheme. Professor Thomas Harrison of the University of Liverpool first suggested the project to me and has been enormously generous throughout; I'm conscious also of my obligations to Duckworth's anonymous reader. Parts of the project have been tried out on audiences in Manchester, Nottingham and Glasgow and I'm grateful for their feedback. And I have learnt much from conversations with Lynn Fotheringham, Jill Harries, Alice Jenkins, Costas Panayotakis, Alison Phipps and Ian Ruffell.

1

Genre

Any assessment of Cicero's achievement as a writer and of the importance of texts to his public character must start with the basic facts of what he wrote. I list in an appendix his known works, dated where possible: even with an author as well-documented as Cicero, there are areas of uncertainty, both in the dating of extant works and in the nature of lost works – and even, in the case of forensic works, of their existence in a written form subsequent to their delivery. But even allowing for these uncertainties, Cicero's corpus is impressive both in scope and in scale. The survival of a large part of Cicero's writings can, however, mislead as to his distinctiveness in both these regards. In this chapter, I want to site Cicero as an author within the late Republican literary context and to argue that what is striking about him is neither simply that he wrote at enormous length, nor that he displays generic flexibility and inventiveness. He is also distinctive in the relentless subordination of text to his public persona and aspirations for political success.

Cicero's works can most straightforwardly be arranged under four generic headings: speeches, poetry, letters, and treatises. Each of these genres had developed at Rome in different ways and at different speeds, and the nature of Cicero's own contribution to the process varies. In each case the loss of much of what had been written earlier makes an assessment of his work speculative: nonetheless, some useful broad parameters can be established.

Speeches

The best established of the kinds of writing which Cicero used was oratory. Roman orators had been writing down their speeches since the early second century: for Cicero, whose history of oratory, *Brutus*, is the source of most of our knowledge of the development of oratory at Rome, Cato the elder is the first significant figure to write down his speeches. Previously, with the exception of a single speech by Appius Claudius Caecus, only funeral speeches had been preserved.[1] Thereafter, dissemination of written versions of speeches became fairly common, and as Cicero trained as an orator in the 90s and 80s, he would have had access to a wide range of recent or contemporary examples.

But while there was a substantial history of writing down speeches, the activity still raised methodological questions. The recording of speeches was not automatic: an orator made a choice whether or not to disseminate a version of what he had said at a trial or in the forum. The relationship between spoken and written speeches has been much discussed, and at the very least it seems improbable that the texts and fragments that survive are exact transcriptions of what was said, however close in general substance and language the two versions were.[2] Moreover, many orators chose never, or very infrequently, to disseminate their speeches, reluctant to produce a permanent record of their beliefs, or skill. M. Antonius, C. Aurelius Cotta and P. Sulpicius – three of the dominant figures when Cicero was a young man – did not leave a single written speech; Cicero tells an anecdote in which Antonius explains that this was because he was afraid of being held to self-contradiction. Hortensius – again we rely on Cicero for the judgement – 'spoke better than he wrote'. Crassus wrote down 'very few' of his speeches, and none of his forensic cases.[3] There was a substantial element among Roman orators, including many of the most effective practitioners, which did not seek to preserve their spoken words. We should not assume, therefore, that there was a clear or obvious course of action for Cicero to take in relation to written dissemination of his oratory.

In other words, once Cicero found himself employed as an advocate he still needed to decide whether and how to record his performances in court. Nor was it a matter of a single decision: over the course of his career he had written versions of only about a half of his speeches disseminated, and it seems that the choice of whether to publish or not was one made afresh each time. Various factors have been put forward to explain Cicero's practice, including the political implications of the case, the obscurity or otherwise of the case, and whether or not he was successful.[4] These observations provide convincing explanations for most of the individual cases, but it is important too to see Cicero's writing in this genre as the conscious creation of a structured record of his career as an orator.

I take it as a given that for Cicero oratory is never simply an end in itself. However brilliant he was as an orator, and however much satisfaction he derived from the position of eminence that he eventually reached in this field, he did not speak just in order to speak. Oratory was a means ultimately to political advancement: and ability as an orator was the chief advantage which Cicero possessed as an aspirant politician. As a forensic orator, Cicero furthered his political ambitions in a variety of ways: specific bonds of obligation with clients and their connections (including the potential for financial gain) were complemented by a more general reputation for competence as a speaker. And in the fiercely competitive and largely unstructured political arena of the late Republic, establishing some form of public profile was an essential preliminary to electoral success. Indeed, the importance of family in this struggle must to a certain extent simply be explained by familiarity: one voted for a Claudius Pulcher or a Cornelius Lentulus not simply or necessarily because one had been paid to do so, or threatened if one did not, but because one recognised the name. Family, that is, was an important badge of identity in a political system where there were no parties to provide that identity ready-made. And for someone whose name did not ring any bells in the minds of a Roman voter, a reputation as an active and successful advocate could be a substitute. This was a reputation which had to be forged in the first place in the forum: but written texts were essential too, both in reaching a wider audience and in establishing a permanent record of what would otherwise be of merely ephemeral note.

It is not a coincidence, then, that Cicero produced written versions of a high proportion of the speeches he delivered at the start of his career, particularly before his election to the praetorship, since it was at this period that the simple act of getting his name known was most important, and when his opportunities to do so outside the courts were most limited. But even at this period there is a divergence between his activity as a speaker and his lasting presence in written form. He did not, it seems, produce written versions of the cases which followed his first criminal case, the defence of Sextus Roscius of Ameria, namely those of a woman from Arretium and of Titinia. Crawford suggests either that his departure for Greece followed too closely, or that he was worried about possible offence to Sulla.[5] Nor did he publish his defence of young Romans in trouble with the draft in Sicily, nor those of Scamander and of Mustius. Scamander was convicted, and Mustius may have been too obscure to have been of interest to anyone else: but nonetheless it is clear that Cicero is discriminating in where to expend effort from the outset of his career as an orator. Before the trial of Verres, Cicero had produced written versions of two criminal trials, that is of Sex. Roscius' trial on a charge of parricide and L. Varenus' on a group of charges of murder and assault; of two civil cases, the property disputes of Quinctius and Tullius (and possibly a third, for Quintus Roscius the actor, though the dating of that speech remains a problem);[6] and the speech he gave as he left Lilybaeum after his quaestorship. In his permanent public record, then, Cicero brought out his capacity to handle both sensational criminal trials and the nitty-gritty of civil trials; the latter might seem dull to modern readers (as they did to Tacitus' interlocutor, Aper, in the *Dialogus* [20]) but it is probable that competent handling of civil cases was as important a means of generating obligations and connections as acting in criminal cases, and such cases were probably also much more frequent. An aspiring orator could not afford to neglect this branch of law, and disseminating written versions of civil cases could be seen as a method of advertising specific services. But it is clear that as aesthetic objects, and as demonstrations of oratorical skill, they had limited appeal; the last such case which Cicero committed to writing was *On behalf of Caecina*, in the year after the trial of Verres.

It is also possible that Cicero was a little more tolerant of failure in writing up his early speeches than later in his career. Apart from *On behalf of Milo*, a special case which I discuss at length in Chapter 4, the only case where Cicero is known to have published a failure is

On behalf of Varenus; and there are good grounds for thinking that he may have lost his very first forensic case, which was published (*On behalf of Quinctius*).[7] Initially, then, any reputation appears to have been more important than a reputation for invariable success; though it may well be the case also that Cicero's efforts on behalf of Varenus, whose case seems to have been nearly hopeless, were very impressive even though they did not lead to acquittal. Certainly Quintilian cites it frequently as a source of examples of good practice.[8]

Cicero's first decade as an orator is, then, presented to the world as a combination of solid diligence with high profile daring. But this should not conceal the fact that his client base in this first decade is not strikingly high-powered: Italian *domi nobiles* for the most part. The support of this group was of course essential to Cicero's electoral success; but he did not also during this period manage to become an advocate for the Roman elite. And members of the elite were in need of good advocates at this period. Nine probable *repetundae* trials are recorded between 80 and 70; there was enormous judicial activity concerning the alleged attempts to poison Cluentius; and there was a scandal involving the Vestal Virgins which generated three attested trials.[9] His breakthrough as an orator is surely to be dated to his prosecution of Verres: and it is indeed possible that a conscious strategy to market himself aggressively as a speaker, as he looked beyond quaestorship and aedileship to the big, and correspondingly remoter, prize of praetorship, lies behind his decision to engage in this potentially dangerous prosecution and one undertaken, moreover, at an unusual period in his career. If Cicero was not getting exciting clients as a defence advocate, then he would have to manufacture his chance by prosecuting: and when his gamble succeeded so magnificently, he responded by producing one of the most substantial oratorical texts yet written in Latin. Is it coincidence that his first senatorial client appeared the following year?[10]

The trial of Verres was also significant because Verres was defended by Hortensius, at that point the leading orator at Rome. Hortensius was consul in the following, and thereafter he retreated from intensive judicial activity for much of the next decade;[11] Cicero seems to have seized the opportunity to secure his position as an orator. From this point onwards he becomes involved in more high-profile forensic cases, such as the trials of the tribunes Manilius and Cornelius, and he also for the first time has the opportunity to address the Roman people, as praetor in 66 BC. This is reflected too in what he chooses to publish. A climax comes in his consulship: not only was this the busiest year of his entire oratorical career, during which he is recorded as having delivered fourteen speeches, but those of which he produced a written version were also eventually shaped into a distinct corpus of consular oratory, a move which I discuss in Chapter 2.

Cicero did not abandon oratory after his consulship and he continued to be active as a defence advocate both before and after his exile in 58-7 BC: but this is not matched, particularly not in the fifties, by such a high proportion of speeches being transformed into written texts. A range of factors are involved in this change. One is that Cicero was simply much busier as an advocate than he had been before his consulship: the absolute number of speeches disseminated is not lower, even though they form a smaller proportion of a now extensive forensic practice, and there must have been a limit to how many speeches Cicero had the time and inclination to write up. Crude self-advertisement was no longer necessary, and as the decade passed, he began to develop other forms of prose writing: there were alternatives to oratory as media for keeping his name before the public. Undoubtedly, too, Cicero chose not to write up a number of the speeches which he gave at the behest of Pompeius: he preferred not to record as part of his oratorical legacy occasions when his involvement in a case was clear evidence of his lack of political autonomy.

Cicero's career as a forensic advocate comes to an end in 52 with the defence of Milo, and as I argue in Chapter 4 the circumstances and content of the written version of that speech mark in themselves a radical transformation. The two ostensibly forensic speeches delivered in front of Caesar, *On behalf of Ligarius* and *On behalf of King Deiotarus*, are different. They were delivered not in front of a jury but to Caesar as sole judge; and the legal framework under which Ligarius and Deiotarus were being charge was opaque.[12]

The *Philippics* are a striking coda to this oratorical narrative. As the textual record of the period in which Cicero was a leading figure in the struggle to maintain the Republic, they are a crucial element in the biographical story-arc: Cicero's final, fatal stand for freedom. But they also transform our view of Cicero as an orator. At the simplest level, they turn Cicero the orator from a figure who belongs overwhelmingly to the courts to one whose skills are more evenly distributed between deliberative and forensic rhetoric. There are about thirty surviving forensic speeches: apart from the fourteen *Philippics*, thirteen deliberative speeches. Moreover, the *Philippics* give a sense of engagement with the nitty-gritty of political life unparalleled in Cicero's other speeches. Seven of them contain the actual texts of decrees which Cicero wishes to have passed; none of Cicero's other senatorial speeches do; and there is a sense too that these speeches are responses to a rapidly developing and complex situation.[13] Here, we might argue, is Cicero engaged in a genuine and sustained attempt to change the course of events through speech: the pendulum of oratory, oscillating between authoritative self-presentation at one end, and dynamic intervention at the other, has swung as far as it can towards making things happen. But, importantly, before we embrace too enthusiastically a narrative of Cicero, at what was to be the end of his career, transcending his concern for self in order to take his place as a leader of men, we should note that the *Philippics* are also textual presences.

In these speeches the need to contribute to senatorial debates is combined with a desire to address a much wider audience, and Cicero is not alone in this. He refers to *edicta*, 'manifestos' or 'proclamations' from Decimus Brutus and Marcus Antonius and speeches from Tiberius Cannutius;[14] much of the thirteenth *Philippic* is a discussion of a letter from Antonius to Hirtius and Octavian; in the second *Philippic* Cicero attacks Antonius for having read aloud in the Senate a letter which he, Cicero, had sent him.[15] This was also a period in which Cicero was engaged in extensive letter-writing with various commanders in the field. I discuss these letters in more detail in Chapter 3, but as an initial point we should observe that it makes sense to see speeches and letters working in tandem: both elements in Cicero's efforts to keep key figures loyal to the Senate and to keep the Senate consistent and effective in its opposition to

Antonius. It is also worth remembering that the second *Philippic* was never delivered: it purports to be Cicero's reply to Antonius' attack on him in the Senate on 19 September, but Cicero was not present at that meeting. And while it is possible that Cicero, in composing a detailed rebuttal of Antonius' charges, worked only from a verbal account of the meeting, or an unofficial written memorandum, Antonius himself probably had a text of his speech disseminated.[16] Texts were flying around. The most striking encapsulation of this is that neither Cicero nor Antonius ever heard the other speak during this period: indeed, their last documented face-to-face encounter is 17 March 44, when both were present in the Senate. The enmity which led to Cicero's death arose from written texts: as the story told of the display of Cicero's head and the right hand which had written the *Philippics* demonstrates.[17]

Cicero's corpus of speeches dominates our view of late Republican oratory to the almost literal exclusion of everything else: but in writing down and disseminating his speeches he was not doing anything particularly different from his contemporaries; his distinctiveness arose from the quality and extent of what he had disseminated. But his other writings do mark out distinctive new ground.

Poetry

Cicero's poetry was the one part of his writing which met with a hostile critical reaction, encapsulated in Aper's remark in Tacitus' *Dialogus* on the poems of Caesar and Brutus: they wrote 'no better than Cicero, but were more fortunate, inasmuch as fewer know that they wrote'.[18] By the time of the Principate, critical opinion was clear: Cicero's poems were a blot on an otherwise distinguished literary record. The genesis and nature of the critical response are considered in the next chapter in the context of Cicero's self-presentation in relation to Catiline; at this point I shall consider only the poetic background and the nature of his contribution to the development of various genres.

Cicero's first poems, including a number of translations, were written as a young man. Plutarch had access to a piece called *Pontius*

Glaucus written when Cicero was 'still a boy' and Cicero himself describes his translation of Aratus' *Phaenomena* as written while he was *admodum adulescentulus*. The exact chronology is impossible to establish, but at any rate these were works written well before Cicero embarked on a public career. *Pontius Glaucus* is known simply from Plutarch's reference: he says it was in tetrameters, which may mean septenarii.[19] Although nothing further is known of Cicero's treatment, the story as told elsewhere concerns a fisherman from Anthedon, opposite Euboea, who ate a magic herb and became a prophetic sea-god; and while it was a 'quintessentially Hellenistic theme', handled by Callimachus, Nicander, and Alexander of Aetolia, it is also the title of a play (probably a satyr-play) by Aeschylus.[20] His handling of Aratus is much clearer, since over 500 lines survive, a considerable proportion of them in a separate manuscript tradition. From the perspective of a literary history of Rome, these works are significant because they demonstrate the importance of 'Hellenistic' poetry well before the generation of Catullus.

Other pieces of poetry that are attested are *Nilus* and *Vxorius*; *Alcyones* (a two-line fragment survives); some lines on Terence in a collection called *Limon*; a hexameter line 'now far and wide the doves the Tyrrhenian sea ...' from a poem in elegiacs with an indecipherable title; a two-line epigram, though the ascription to Cicero is doubtful on metrical grounds; a poem on *His consulship* (*Consulatus suus*), in hexameters; a poem on Marius, also in hexameters; and a poem *On his vicissitudes* (*de temporibus suis*) concerning his exile and return, of which he seems to have composed at least two books, but which was probably never disseminated.[21] Of these, the only ones which can be dated with any certainty are *His consulship* (written during 60) and *On his vicissitudes* (in progress between 56 and 54). The composition of these two can be dated with fair precision as a result of Cicero's references to them in his letters, and the absence of references to other pieces of poetry in the letters could be used as an argument for their composition being early and thus before Cicero's surviving correspondence.

But the time of composition is not necessarily the same as time of dissemination. In the late 50s, when he wrote *On the laws*, Cicero drew attention to his poem on Marius: a particular oak tree at

Arpinum, and its connection, or lack of it, with Marius as described by Cicero in this work provides the subject of the opening exchange in the dialogue. But there is no way to tell from this passage, or from a quotation from it in *On divination*, whether Cicero had recently composed the poem, or whether he had composed it much earlier, nor how long Atticus had had access to it.[22] There is an argument for placing its composition after Cicero's return from exile, on the grounds that this point of similarity between Marius and Cicero made Marius a much more resonant figure for Cicero than he had been before, as the greater number of references in the speeches show; and one might question too whether Cicero would wish to stress his relationship with Marius earlier (certainly he seems to avoid exploiting the connection as a young man).[23] But ultimately the decision depends on how one views Cicero's writing of poetry, and more importantly perhaps, how far one thinks that his writing of poetry must, at any point in his career, be uniform: that is, how far one wants to believe he wrote mythological poetry (and *only* mythological poetry) as a young man, and in his middle age wrote autobiographical and political poetry (and *only* autobiographical and political poetry).

If a chronology of Cicero's poetry is fraught with difficulty, so is drawing conclusions about the nature of his work. But some trends are apparent. Productive speculation about *Nilus* and *Vxorius* is difficult, since nothing beyond their titles is known; and a wider context for the line about doves is difficult to supply. But *Alcyones* presumably told the story of Ceyx and Alcyone and their transformation into sea-birds – making this, together with *Pontius Glaucus*, the earliest metamorphosis poem in Latin; it was a story told by Nicander in his *Metamorphoses* . It would be reasonable to conclude that, as a young man, Cicero had access to and read a range of Greek poetry of the third century BC, which is conventionally called 'Hellenistic', and that his interest led him to a considerable effort in translation; he may also, if *Alcyones* and *Pontius Glaucus* were not simply translations, have experimented with original work in a variety of meters which took less familiar mythological stories as a starting point, a type of narrative which imitated some of the verse which he read.

1. Genre

This is a Roman engagement with Hellenistic poetry a quarter of a century before Catullus and his contemporaries produced their work; and Cicero's work can be related, in a necessarily speculative fashion, to other writing in the first two decades of the first century. There are the erotic epigrams, based on Hellenistic originals, which Gellius quotes (*N.A.* 19.9), and Laevius appears to be writing mythological narrative poetry at this period, though his work is impossible to date precisely.[24] Plutarch's observation that, as a young man, Cicero was considered to be the best poet at Rome, cannot be dismissed on the grounds that Cicero was working in a poetic desert; nor is his achievement simply a matter of improving the hexameter, though his accomplishment in the metrical field is considerable. In subject matter, too, he seems to have been at the forefront of a new interest in more recent Greek poetry and in the possibilities of transferring and adapting it in Latin.

It remains to consider the nature of the composition and dissemination of this category of Cicero's poetry, that is, those works which are derived in some way from Hellenistic originals and whose subject matter does not relate to contemporary events. It is possible that there is an element of practice and exercise in their composition: the case has been made that Cicero's epigram on Terence was written at the behest of Antonius Gnipho, with whom he studied up to his praetorship. And it is possible to see how the discipline of translating a difficult and recherché text might appeal to Cicero as a means of exercising and perfecting his verbal facility. Nor need dissemination initially have meant anything more than making a copy of a piece judged to be successful and giving it to one or more friends or acquaintances who shared Cicero's interest in this type of poetry. But a small-scale and intimate model of dissemination, and one which was entirely non-commercial, should not be taken to preclude Cicero's having an interest in his reputation among a wider group of readers. He certainly seems to have gained one: in addition to Plutarch's remark specifically about his poetry there are various anecdotes which suggest that he acquired a distinctive profile as someone with an interest in and fondness for Greek culture, and his poetry was presumably part of the basis for this.[25]

Although it is not clear that there must be a distinct divide in

31

Cicero's poetry writing between early, mythological, Hellenistic poetry and late autobiographical work, the work he started on in 60 is utterly distinctive. It marks the coalescing of two distinct genres. On the one hand, there is the tradition of poetry about the achievements of the poet's patron: Ennius accompanied Fulvius Nobilior on his campaigns in Ambracia in the 180s, though the work which emerged may have been a play rather than an epic poem; Hostius wrote a *Bellum Histricum*, probably about the campaigns of C. Sempronius Tuditanus in 129; Furius Antias probably wrote on Catulus' Cimbrian command.[26] And this tradition was not confined to poetry in Latin: the immediate cause of Cicero's turning to composition was that his hope of a poem about himself, in Greek, from Archias, who had celebrated Lucullus, was evaporating. On the other hand, there is the genre of the prose memoir, as practised, among others, by Aemilius Scaurus, Rutilius Rufus and Sulla.[27] Cicero's distinctive move was to use the form of hexameter epic in order to write autobiography, with its well-established tolerance for partial and self-serving narrative.

As I discuss in Chapter 2, Cicero's decision to forge this new kind of poetry arises directly from his anxieties about his position in the aftermath of the Catilinarian conspiracy: and it is not the only form of writing he uses at this time to promote his reputation. Nonetheless, it is also clear from the surviving fragments and testimonia of *His consulship* that he readily employed the distinctive features of epic narration and by so doing attempted to present himself in heroic guise: there was a council of the gods, to which Cicero was summoned, and at least twice he was addressed by a Muse.[28] The work seems also to have been philosophically informed: the description of Jupiter in the longest surviving fragment clearly draws on Stoic conception of the divine mind, and the work's emphasis on divination also fits a Stoic framework.

This blending of genres enabled Cicero to craft a form of self-presentation which transcended the constraints of prose memoirs while keeping the message entirely under his own control. Nor should the hostile reception of the poem – and *His consulship* is the piece largely responsible for Cicero's poor reputation as a poet – detract from the force of the message he was attempting to transmit. The surviving fragments show that Cicero presented the threat posed by the Catilinarian conspiracy as a matter which disturbed the normal course of events for years in advance;[29] the conspirators were impelled to action by their own moral depravity;[30] Cicero gave Rome a new birth through his civilian leadership;[31] his actions received divine approval, and he is commanded to continue in the same path: 'Meanwhile, keep to the courses which you have followed with courage and intelligence from your earliest youth until your consulship and increase your reputation and the esteem of good men'.[32] The scope of epic allowed Cicero to fashion an integrated vision of himself and the city of Rome as elements within a divinely ordered and harmonious cosmos: an image whose persuasiveness we can only glimpse from the fragments of the poem which remain.

Treatises

Over the course of his career Cicero had disseminated some twenty-five or so prose works other than speeches. One straightforward way of classifying these works is into those on rhetoric, and those on philosophy; but while this has the benefit of simplicity, it misrepresents the range of Cicero's interests and the variety that can be seen within the philosophica and rhetorica.

One element in the problem is that a number of prose works that Cicero wrote, which do not fall into either category, are lost. Specifically, he wrote: a brief prose summary, in Greek, of his consulship, a *commentarius* designed to be worked up by another, and there may also have been a version in Latin; a laudatory memoir of Cato; and a funeral oration for Porcia. In 59 he contemplated writing a geographical work, though there is no evidence that this ever went beyond the conceptual stage.[33] This range of kinds of writing demonstrates that any view of Cicero's treatise writing as something which involves simply rhetorical and philosophical works is seriously misleading. Moreover, with the exception of the work on geography, these are pieces which arise directly from contemporary events. I discuss the memoir of his consulship in Chapter 2, as part of a multi-faceted assault on his reputation in relation to the Catilinarian conspiracy. The others are from the period of Caesar's dictatorship, and all fit a model of literary activity which has Cicero looking for ways of continuing to comment on public affairs in a situation in which oratory has ceased to be a rewarding form, inasmuch as the courts were suspended, the Senate had ceased to be a genuine deliberative assembly and he had no access to the people. Cato's suicide provoked a rash of attempts to make sense of his life and death, above all in relation to his implacable hostility to Caesar;[34] and in addition to joining this debate Cicero quite possibly continued it in his fictional funeral oration for Cato's sister.

The literary response to Cato's death marks a new turn in the tradition of posthumous accounts of famous men inasmuch as the act of commemoration is not restricted to the immediate family. It was not the first time that politicians had used the funeral oration as a means to self-promotion, but hitherto they had relied upon the fortuitous decease of their own relatives: Caesar's own oration for his aunt Julia is the example frequently cited. In these cases, too, the speech was not necessarily the main focus of the commemoration: funeral games, with their opportunities for spectacle and largesse, were often more important. But the record of Cato's death both extended beyond his relatives, to become a subject which could be treated by anyone; and shifted the act of remembrance from the sphere of public performance to scattered debating by means of written texts. This paradox – that the death of an individual became a matter of enormous concern outside his family while being deprived of the ceremonies which had previously enabled private grief and loss to become a site for universal participation – arose from Cato's own position, as the defender of a *res publica* which had ceased to exist. And Caesar himself participated in the debate with the composition of his *Anti-Cato*. He was at the forefront of those seeking to exploit the potential in the transformation of Rome from city-state to cosmopolis, and the implications of that for the spread of information.

In these works, then, Cicero was part of a wider movement among the elite who were attempting to find new ways of discussing the *res publica* and their place within it. But a creative approach to the possibilities of prose texts is a feature of his writing career from the outset, and the two surviving categories of rhetorical and philosophical works conceal a huge variety of kinds of writing. His first prose work was *On invention*, a rhetorical handbook of an entirely conventional kind. At first sight this can appear to be Cicero's least interesting work: a treatise on how to find material for speeches, elaborated in enormous detail. As a guide to actual rhetorical practice it is overshadowed by the roughly contemporary *Rhetoric to Herennius*, which surpasses it both in clarity and in comprehensiveness (the latter covers all five of the parts of oratory and not simply, as Cicero's, one): both important qualities in a textbook. But it would be a mistake to dismiss *On invention* as a dull piece of juvenilia, since it provides a unique way into Cicero's aspirations at the start of his adult life.[35]

We do not know when *On invention* was composed. The only evidence for its dissemination comes at the opening of the first book of *On the orator*, where Cicero says, addressing the work's dedicatee, his brother Quintus,

> For you want, as you have often told me, something about these matters [sc. the art of speaking] which is rather more polished and finished by me, seeing as those rough and unpolished things which fell out of my notebooks when I was a boy, or rather young man, are scarcely worthy of my years now and of the experience which I have attained in the large number of important cases that I have pleaded.[36]

On invention is the only known candidate for the 'rough and unpolished' work: and *On the orator* is being presented as a replacement for it, which will reflect Cicero as the successful orator that he has become in place of the boy or young man who wrote *On invention* and which itself, it is suggested, was an unfinished student work.

But this apparently straightforward piece of literary history is arguably somewhat disingenuous. In the first place, it is rather vague on chronology: does the disjunction between 'boy' and 'young man' indicated a period on the cusp between the two ages, or is it rather an act of self-correction, in keeping with the informal conversational tone of the opening chapters? Cicero's words would be consistent with any time from his mid-teens until his early twenties or even beyond: *adulescentia* is a flexible concept, and on occasion can refer to men around the age of forty. In this case, it is improbable that the *On invention* was written after Cicero delivered his first speech in 81, but we are still left with the decade between 91 and 81.[37] This was a period not without incident in Cicero's life. By 89 he was fighting in the Social war in Pompeius Strabo's army, and then with Sulla. Subsequently he was at Rome during the period of Cinna's power and there, or at any rate in Italy, during Sulla's invasion and capture of the city.

Throughout this period Cicero would have been uncertain about the nature and extent of any public career that might become open to him. His background, as a member of an Italian family, important in its own area but not hitherto involved in politics at Rome, imposed limits on realistic ambitions. The Cicerones had connections with a number of figures among the elite, but as a new man who was not, in relative terms, outstandingly wealthy, Cicero lacked two of the most important keys to political success, birth and money. In their absence, an aspiring politician needed to acquire a reputation in other ways, and the two most important were military activity and oratory. Cicero did try being a soldier, but we know very little about his experiences. He refers only twice to his military experiences in his subsequent writing: a reference to a conference between Pompeius Strabo and the leader of the Marsi, Vettius Scato; and to an act of divination in Cornelius Sulla's army while it was attacking the Samnites.[38] Neither episode involved combat, nor indeed any action by Cicero beyond spectating. But what is unanswerable is that Cicero avoided every subsequent chance to be a soldier, until he was sent, reluctantly, to Cilicia. It is fair to conclude that whatever happened to Cicero in the army during the Social war convinced him either that he did not want to be a soldier, or that he did not have the skills to make a serious mark in the field. With this option tried and rejected, there was nothing to distract him from oratory.

However, there was a problem with the practice of oratory from 87 BC onwards. This was the period of the military dictatorship of Marius and Cinna, whose takeover of Rome was accompanied by a massacre of their opponents, including Marcus Antonius, Quintus

Catulus and Caesar Strabo, and a cessation of lawcourt activity.[39]
Moreover, it would not have been clear from the perspective of the
mid-80s what the future might hold and, in particular, what the
opportunities for participation in public life might be. While one
should not exaggerate the extent to which previous patterns of life
were disrupted by Cinna, nonetheless Cicero's hopes for advancement must have looked very different after Marius had seized power.
And behind everything in Rome during these years was the distant
figure of Sulla and the inevitable prospect of his return to Italy.

In these circumstances, Cicero cultivated his intellectual interests
more widely. He studied philosophy with Philo of Larissa, the head
of the Academy who arrived in Rome in 88 BC and with Diodotus,
as well as rhetoric with Milo of Rhodes; and he practised declamation in both Latin and Greek.[40] In *Brutus*, he presents this training
as something which eventually enabled him to start his oratorical
career fully trained, rather than having to learn on the job, as most
people did (311). But at the time the uses to which his knowledge
might be put would have seemed more opaque. And I would suggest
that Cicero's composition of *On invention* and his dissemination of
this text should be seen in this context, as the work of an ambitious
and highly intelligent young man, whose hopes for a part in public
life at Rome were uncertain. Even if *On invention* predates the Social
war, it can still be seen as a demonstration of ability and commitment
in a field of knowledge central to Roman life; and if its composition
does belong to the 80s then it fulfils this role even more emphatically,
given that Cicero had by then tried and rejected the other obvious
career, as a soldier, and his opportunities within the civilian sphere
were now restricted not only by his background but also by the
continuing political uncertainty. Nor should one doubt the work's
ambition on the grounds that it is likely only to have circulated
among a small number, or indeed that it may never have been
designed for circulation. Cicero's remark in *On the orator* about its
slipping from his notebooks is disingenuous, and an attempt to raise
one's profile within a small and relatively close-knit elite, as at Rome,
and one where the political and literary worlds are closely entwined,
need have involved only a dozen or fewer copies. And a considera-

tion of the nature of the work itself shows that this is not at all an unpolished piece.

Whether Cicero's *On invention* is in fact the first example in Latin of a rhetorical handbook is unanswerable, given the problem of its dating relative to the *Rhetoric to Herennius*; but there does not seem to be anything predating these two works.[41] On the basis of the similarities and divergences between the two works it is unlikely that the subsequent writer borrowed from his predecessor – though this does not preclude knowledge of the previous work's existence.[42] It is reasonable, then, to see in *On invention* an ambition which is perhaps now obscured by the apparently drab form of a technical treatise. The material in it is not original: so much would be clear even without the close similarity of the *Rhetoric to Herennius*. But it is one of the first attempts to put into written Latin form a systematic account of rhetoric.

Cicero's intellectual self-confidence in this work comes to the fore in the prefaces to the two books. In book one, he considers and justifies the study of rhetoric in a well-ordered state, and in book two he explains his eclectic use of sources and offers a brief history of (Greek) rhetorical writing. Neither of these sections is paralleled in the *Rhetoric to Herennius*, in which only the first book contains prefatory remarks, and these are brief and related to the author's motives in writing. Cicero's style in the two prefaces is polished and elaborate. In the first, he offers a history of the development of civilisation which is strikingly similar to the accounts offered in the Greek philosophical tradition and then considers the scope of the art of rhetoric, with reference to examples of Gorgias and Aristotle as well as to Hermagoras, whose *stasis*-system was the basis of Cicero's scheme of rhetoric. In the second book, he uses an anecdote about the painter Zeuxis as an introduction into his defence of his method, which he claims has involved selecting the best from a wide range of authorities; and he then offers an account of writing on rhetoric which distinguishes between the contributions of philosophers, with Aristotle as the named example, and teachers of rhetoric, represented above all by Isocrates. He concludes this second preface with an acknowledgement of his own lack of dogmatism and willingness to be corrected:

38

It is not being ignorant which is shameful, but in persisting stupidly in one's ignorance, particularly since ignorance is a weakness common to all men, but obstinacy is a vice of an individual. Therefore, I shall proceed with my enquiries without making positive assertions, and shall say things with an element of hesitation, in case in seeking to seem to have written a useful book I lose that most important object, not to agreed to anything in a rash or arrogant way.[43]

It would perhaps be going too far to claim that this passage demonstrates that the composition of *On invention* must belong to the 80s, after Cicero had begun to study philosophy seriously; but at any rate, even if it is earlier, it points forward to the direction his intellectual sympathies were subsequently to develop.

On invention is an enormously self-confident and ambitious work which articulates the Hellenistic rhetorical treatise in Latin form, quite possibly for the first time, and furnishes technical instruction with a bold statement both of the importance of oratory within civil society and of the author's own claims to rhetorical knowledge and proficiency. Moreover, Cicero's work acts out a claim to authority despite the author's lack of personal experience. This is not something that Cicero draws attention to, but, on the assumption that copies circulated with his name on the text – and there is no reason to think that this was not the case, or at least that the modes of textual circulation at this period really allowed for initial dissemination to be anonymous – a reader would know that they did not know of the writer as a practitioner at Rome, though the name clearly indicated a Roman citizen and not a Greek intellectual. This too marks a divergence from the normal profile of the Latin treatise-writer at this point to be drawing on his own actions in his writing, be it as a jurist, in the cases of Scaevola and Manilius and Junius, as a landowner, or as an orator. Even Aelius Stilo had a public profile to the extent of writing speeches for others – an activity which was well known enough to generate his *cognomen*. A twenty-year-old Cicero does not fit into this pattern. And *On invention* may also mark a conscious attempt to effect a synthesis between the conflicting forces of Latin practice and Greek theory; a question which had become a focus of particular debate with the censors' edict in 92 against Latin schools of rhetoric. Cicero himself confesses to the attraction he felt as a young man towards instruction in Latin;[44] and it would certainly accord with my interpretation of *On invention* as a work making enormous intellectual claims if it is also attempting to provide an answer to this problem, or at least a demonstration that a synthesis is possible, and even desirable.

On invention is a calling-card from Cicero to the Roman governing elite. He might have preferred to enter the public arena by means of a spectacular early debut in the forum, but if that was impossible, or unwise, then a demonstration of theoretical competence was a useful substitute.

Cicero's other treatises are very different works. Not only are they, in themselves, discursive and reflective pieces, which eschew the straightforwardly didactic manner of *On invention* in favour of complex expositions of rhetorical and philosophical topics and are self-conscious of their being works by Cicero; but they are also products of a greatly expanded intellectual landscape. It is difficult to trace the contours with any certainty, given the loss of almost everything except Cicero's own works; but one can at least point to the writing that is attested in the thirty years since *On invention*. Particularly important for the treatises of the mid-50s are the works dealing with public affairs at Rome. In addition to the autobiographical prose memoirs mentioned above in relation to *His consulship*, Sisenna had written a history of the Social war and subsequent civil war, which Cicero felt transcended all earlier Latin historiography; Lucceius covered the same period in a work apparently finished by 56, though the date of its dissemination is less clear;[45] Hortensius too had written on the Social war, though possibly in verse. Nepos' *Chronica* were probably already in the public domain, since Catullus knows of them. Although most of Varro's voluminous output was still to come, he had written a a guide for Pompeius to the workings of the Senate; and L. Aurunculeius Cotta had written on the Roman constitution. Cicero himself had contributed with his brief account of his consulship, and Atticus had written a work on the same theme; and it is possible that the first books of Caesar's *commentarii* were already circulating, though there are considerable difficulties with a model of annual circulation.[46]

The tradition, therefore, that public affairs were recorded by those who had participated in them continued to flourish. And this is in contrast with the relative dearth of other forms of prose writing in Latin. There was no geographical writing, though Atticus tried to persuade Cicero to do something in this field in 59. The only prose philosophy in Latin attested was some Epicurean works: Cicero's contempt for them relates to style, it seems, as well as content.[47] The obvious choice for Cicero, if he wished to write something in prose other than speeches, would have been something broadly historical – as indeed his flurry of work after the Catilinarian conspiracy attests. Instead, in the mid-50s, he chooses to write a three-volume dialogue about oratory drawing on Plato and, it seems, Aristotle, for his formal models, in *On the orator*; a six-volume discussion of the Roman state, *On the state*; and a work on its legal system and traditions, *On the laws*. Moreover, he appears to be aware that his not writing history is worthy of comment: at the beginning of *On the laws* Atticus is made to say, 'A work of history has been asked of you – or rather demanded – for a long time now'. A discussion between the three interlocutors then follows in which they consider whether Cicero should take a contemporary subject or the more distant past; he emphatically opts for the former, but then argues that he does not have time, at present, for such a work.[48]

The reasons for Cicero's choice are opaque, and it is possibly futile even to speculate on why he eschewed history. Nor should one disregard entirely the excuses he made in *On the laws*, that the writing of history required concentrated labour of a sort different from that which could produce his other work. Nonetheless, he had already, at the time of this *recusatio*, engaged in fairly substantial historical research in order to create the accurate settings of *On the orator* and *On the state*, and had included brief portions of historical narrative in them, particularly the description of Crassus' final speech and death at the beginning of book 3 of *On the orator*. And this is the key point. Almost all of Cicero's treatises are located at a specified time and place and among a historically possible group of people. I discuss the mechanics and implications of these *mises-en-*

scène in Chapter 3: here I would suggest some broader implications of Cicero's decision.

A dominant theme in Roman historiography was military activity: hence any piece of conventional Roman history that Cicero wrote would inevitably involve his own part in events being sidelined; and it would perhaps also be arguable that he did not have the qualifications necessary to write that kind of history. At the very least, historiography greater in scale than the monograph of a kind which Cicero had already written would draw attention to his somewhat unusual public career. Or, to put the problem in another form: arguably what Cicero is attempting to do in the three treatises of the late 50s is to engage in the kind of writing about public affairs drawn from personal experience that was so well-established, but to do so in a fashion appropriate to his own skills and activities. Thus his first substantial prose work is not a conventional narrative of war and politics but a reflection upon the nature of the civilian public figure; and, as I argue in Chapter 2, one of its concerns is to redefine the nature of civilian public activity in order to encompass the figure of the 'politician', that is to create a role for a man constantly engaged in guiding the deliberations of the state, regardless of whether or not he actually held a magistracy.

That the treatises of the 50s are, in part, an attempt to create a form of historiography which fits with the imperatives of Cicero's own experience, must remain a hypothesis; it is clearer that they are also an attempt to express Greek philosophical argument in Latin.[49] The scale of the philosophical achievement in the treatises of the 40s has perhaps tended to draw attention away from this aspect of the three, given the distinction between philosophical and rhetorical works; but the earlier treatises too are profoundly philosophical in form and content. They are the beginning of a process of naturalising philosophy into Latin which is continued and completed by the treatises of the Caesarian period, as the catalogue in the second book of *On divination* indicates: it includes *On the orator* and *On the state* (though not *On the laws*, an indication that it was never formally disseminated). The difference between the works before and after the outbreak of civil war in 49 lies not so much in whether or not they are philosophical but rather in the choice of topics within philosophy. To generalise: in the 50s, Cicero is using the tools of philosophy in order to reflect upon his own position within the state. During Caesar's dictatorship, the creation of a philosophical literature in Latin has itself become the end, that is, the most effective way in which he can fulfil his public duties. And it is notable that after Caesar's death, Cicero's treatise-writing shows a swing back towards topics which could be seen as relevant to the Republican public figure: glory, friendship and duty.

Letters

The remaining division of Cicero's writing is his letters. As I indicated in the Introduction, this is the most difficult part of the corpus from the perspective of this study because of the nature of dissemination: are they not private? But there are two respects in which the letters may not be private. One is the vulnerability of correspondence to outside scrutiny, either with the permission of the recipient (s/he shows it to a third party) or without (the letter is tampered with en route). The other is the fact that the sender may want the letter to be shown to other people, or at least not object if this happens. But it would also be a mistake to assume that in those parts of the correspondence where Cicero hoped for privacy he had no regard at all for the impression that his letter might create on a wider audience.

In fact, it is not that letters are irrelevant to this enquiry, but that they are so fundamental a means of existing within the public sphere that they sidestep the elaborate structures which enable Cicero to use other types of writing as a means of projecting his public personae. Whereas in the speeches, poetry or treatises Cicero is demonstrating either skill in performance, as an orator, or as a authoritative public figure who is thereby in a position to discourse upon weighty matters of public or intellectual concern, or is drawing attention to the message which is conveyed in these enticing packages, his letters are unmediated acts of persuasion: but ones whose audience may be no greater than a single person.

Closer scrutiny of the notion of dissemination as it relates to correspondence will show that the letters only become difficult in the terms of this work if one holds to an unnecessarily rigid idea of 'publication'. But it is also important to be clear about the nature of the corpus of letters as a whole, since they are by no means a unified whole: four separate collections survive. There are sixteen volumes of letters from Cicero to Atticus, from the years 65-44; three to his brother Quintus from the 50s; twenty-six letters between Cicero and Brutus from the spring and summer of 43; and sixteen volumes of letters to and from Cicero and a miscellaneous range of correspondents, from immediately after the end of his consulship down to the summer of 43. A few fragments of other letters also survive, and there are references to other collections which have not survived.[50]

When and how the work of collection and editing happened is not clear, though it all belongs to the period after Cicero's death. It is very likely indeed that the letters to Atticus came into the public domain by a different route, and later, than those to other addressees, and that the other letters were edited by Tiro;[51] but whatever the details – and they are irrecoverable – we have here the accumulation of historical artefacts, which, for the initial editors, derived their interest and value from a great figure of the recent past. There is a revealing comment on the letters to Atticus in Nepos' *Life of Atticus*, where he says 'As evidence for this [sc. the affection between Atticus and Cicero], apart from the books in which he [Cicero] mentions him which are in the public domain, there are eleven rolls of letters to Atticus, from his consulate up until his final days; and whoever reads them would not have much need for a continuous history of that period'.[52] This remark is relevant both for the genesis of the *ad Atticum* collection and for Nepos' calibre as a historian; but it also indicates that the process of turning the letters into historical evidence which should be treated as a different way from Cicero's other writings had begun within a few years of his death.

But there are other factors which point in a different direction. It is significant that Cicero himself contemplated in July 44 bringing out a collection of his letters.[53] While there is no evidence that this plan was carried out or that it had any discernible effect on the collections as subsequently arranged, it does demonstrate that Cicero thought that some, at least, of his letters, were potentially suitable for a wider audience than the original recipients. Among the surviving works the idea is mentioned only in this one letter to Atticus:

there Cicero says that Tiro has about 70 letters, and needs a few back from Atticus.[54] He, Cicero, will look over the letters and 'correct' them; thereafter they will be disseminated. There is no sign here that Cicero intended to consult any of the original recipients before wider dissemination; nor is there any indication of the nature of the collection, nor indeed of the amount of editorial interference Cicero intended before dissemination. Was it intended as a collection of historically important documents, of the sort that subsequent editors saw in the letters? Was it to be an epistolary portrait of Cicero, demonstrating his relationships with the dominant figures of the state? Or was it rather to contain the more 'literary' letters, such as those to Marius or the letters of recommendation, a collection of pieces of good writing whose appeal to the reader might lie not simply in political details? It is tempting to read significance into the timing of the plan, that is in the immediate aftermath of Caesar's assassination, as Cicero once more contemplated the possibility of genuine political engagement; but without knowing what was in the collection, it is difficult to come to any conclusions about the nature of that significance. All we can be sure of is that Cicero had come to think that some of his letters were worth disseminating.

That others beyond the original recipients might be interested in Cicero's correspondence is surely not a surprising idea, and is one moreover that Cicero had to take account of in writing. It is one of the essential facts about the epistolary process that one can never be sure that a letter will only be read by its addressee: there is the possibility both of interception, and of the intended recipient's showing a letter to other people. In Cicero's attack on Marcus Antonius in the second *Philippic* he complains bitterly that Antonius has done exactly that: he has made public a private letter from Cicero:

But this boorish fellow, who doesn't understand the conventions of civilised life, has recited a letter which he says I sent him. Does anybody who has the slightest sense of how to behave openly read out and make public a letter which a friend has sent him, even if there's been some quarrel in the mean time? What is this, other than to destroy companionship, to destroy conversations with absent friends? There tend to be lots of jokes in letters, which seem silly if they come out, and lots of serious things which should never be made public.[55]

Cicero proceeds to argue that he could deny authorship, if he wanted, because the letter is not in his own handwriting; and the habit of using secretaries for correspondence added a further level of complication to this form of communication. There is plenty of evidence within the letters themselves that Cicero was worried about security in transmission, and sometimes took account of that in what he wrote; and that forgery was conceivable.[56] Even in the normal course of events letters could not be guaranteed private; and the distinction between 'private' and 'public' in relation to writing is itself much less stable in Cicero's period that we are perhaps conditioned to imagine by the nature of publishing today. When planned and intentional dissemination initially relies upon a personal network of acquaintances and the production of a small number of copies under one's own supervision, and where the delay between completion and dissemination is short, and may depend only on the time taken physically to make a copy, then the distinction between how these works circulate and how a letter might circulate is much smaller than between a letter or email nowadays, which still retains these qualities of personal relationship and of speed, and a work that is 'published' and therefore generated and spread by a complex, impersonal, and slow process.

Moreover, some at least of the letters were intended for a wider audience from the very start of the compositional process. Perhaps the most obvious example is the letter, now lost, to Pompeius, which I discuss in Chapter 2; this was quoted by the prosecutor at a trial a few months after it was sent, apparently as though the letter had been in wide circulation from the time that it had been sent to Pompeius. A set of rather different examples is that of the letters of recommendation, where there is always a third party, that is whoever is being recommended in the letter. Indeed, in Cicero's letters of recommendation the network of obligation and gratitude often spreads even further, as I discuss in Chapter 3. But the point to stress at this stage is that Cicero's letters are enormously varied and that variation includes the extent to which a letter is permeable by those other than the recipient: his letters range from the disguised pamphlet, designed for a wide readership, through formal letters to political equals, on whose discretion Cicero could not necessarily rely, and letters to friends which Cicero might expect to be passed on to further mutual acquaintances, to letters to close friends discussing confidential matters where, one must assume, Cicero fervently hoped that the letter would not be read by any but the recipient.

Moreover, the letters are also the part of Cicero's correspondence where earlier writing in the genre might seem to be of least relevance. There was indeed a firmly-established tradition of letters from magistrates in the field to the Senate; and Cicero's *Verrines* gives a fine insight into the way that letters were essential to business transactions. But this latter kind of letter is ultimately as various as the matters with which it deals.[57] What is perhaps worth noting is that some letters had already become widely disseminated artefacts: the most striking example are the letters of Cornelia to her sons Tiberius and Gaius Gracchus. Some fragments of these are preserved in the manuscripts of Corneius Nepos, and Cicero had access to them when he was writing *Brutus*; regardless of whether or not they were genuine, the fact that something was circulating in this guise indicates an interest in private letters, presumably fuelled here by the notoriety of the recipients.[58] This tradition was presumably an element in Cicero's contemplation of bringing out a collection of his own letters.

The very range of ways in which Cicero uses letters can make it difficult to formulate useful general frameworks for understanding them: it is perhaps not surprising that this is the least studied part of the Ciceronian corpus.[59] In Chapter 3 I suggest that one way to see the letters as manifestations of Cicero's public persona is as key elements in his building communities: that is, in establishing and maintaining the networks of relationships which were at the heart of Cicero's conception of his public role.

The limits of genre

What is the value in thinking about Cicero's writings from a generic point of view? Are the genre-based approaches of much work on

Cicero satisfactory? There is undoubtedly an element of practicality in this approach, as it provides a means of ordering one of the most substantial bodies of material by a single author from the ancient world. And there are sets of information which certain types of writing need to be understood. Clearly, an understanding of ancient rhetoric helps to form expectations of a speech; a knowledge of hexameter poetry informs how we read Cicero's epic fragments; and so forth. And again, there are certain sorts of questions about Cicero's practice whose answers will only draw on parts of his oeuvre: for example, the handling of witnesses, or the use of dialogue form. But beyond these relatively simple observations, I suggest that concerns with genre may in fact impede an understanding of what Cicero is trying to accomplish in any particular work.

This survey of how Cicero's writings relate to their literary context indicates the extent of his creativity and freedom from constraints. The most clearly established of the formats he used was that of the speech. But even there one of the recurrent features in much scholarship of the speeches is the sense that the 'rules' of rhetoric were constantly being disregarded when it suited him, and his use of language became the focus of heated debates on style.[60] He transcended and renewed the expectations of the genre. His use of the epistolary format is so flexible that generic constraints hardly apply (though it is worth noting one almost unbreakable rule of Ciceronian correspondence – politeness).[61] But in his poetry, insofar as we can tell, and certainly in his treatises, he is constantly testing out new possibilities and creating new forms of writing. And related to this generic freedom there is a singular lack of overt anxiety about predecessors and rivals, largely because there are none.

Different forms of writing are, for Cicero, about multiplying possibilities for conveying a particular message: whatever his circumstances, there is always a type of writing that is available. He moves with enormous freedom among them because he lacks inhibition about his capacities to tackle a particular type of writing, and because his ultimate concern is not to be an epic poet, or a philosopher, or even a great orator, but to subsume and incorporate all these textual presences into a permanent record of 'Cicero'. Let us turn now to consider this figure of Cicero.

2

Cicero as a Public Figure

The first chapter set the scene for this study by examining the whole of Cicero's work in terms of literary form and history, and argued that what is distinctive about his writing from this perspective is its variety and flexibility. From this chapter onwards I focus rather on what he is attempting to do in these texts, starting with his self-presentation as a public figure.[1] The key event here is his consulship in 63, because of the range of writings which he uses in the immediate aftermath to record events, particularly the suppression of the Catilinarian conspiracy, and his part in them. We can see Cicero employing his verbal facility in an enormous range of texts and using his skill to solve the problem he had, that other people would not write about him in the ways that he wanted; by breaking down the distinction between who does and who records by performing both roles he can control his image in a wide variety of texts.

In this period he emphasises heroic solitude; after his return from exile he is rather one among many, a devoted servant of the state whose position gains in authority and credibility precisely because it is shared by so many others. This can be traced in the speeches he gave in the aftermath of his return; one can also see in the treatises of the late 50s an attempt to formulate an idea of a public figure which will validate and strengthen what Cicero is attempting to do.

The consul

Cicero was obsessed with the record of his own consulship. His attempts to have this year preserved in text offer a case study of the means and methods of memorialisation as well as indicating what in particular Cicero wished to preserve of his year in office.

49

Our view of Cicero's consulship is, of course, dominated by the events of the final two months of his term of office: the showdown between Cicero and Catiline over Catiline's alleged plans for a violent uprising, Catiline's departure from Rome, the discovery of communications between followers of Catiline and the envoys from the Gaulish tribe of the Allobroges and the execution of five conspirators, on the basis of the letters between them which Cicero discovered.[2] But it is important to bear in mind that the Catilinarian conspiracy was only one of the events of the year. Actually holding the highest magistracy was, on its own, eminently worth recording for any politician, and even more so for one who thereby ennobled his family. Moreover, the first ten months of the consulship of Cicero and Antonius were not without incident. We should not, therefore, assume that the conspiracy would dominate the way in which Cicero chose to record his consulship; indeed, how to treat Catiline was only one of the issues about which Cicero needed to make a decision.

We can trace Cicero's initial efforts at self-memorialisation in four genres: oratory, poetry, letters and historiography. 63 was one of Cicero's more prolific years as an orator: in addition to his forensic activities – the defences of Gaius Rabirius, Gaius Piso and Murena – there were a variety of more directly political debates to which he contributed *qua* consul: Rullus' agrarian law proposal, the political rights of the children of those proscribed by Sulla, seating in the theatre and the disposition of provinces, as well as the Catilinarian problem. Moreover, he regarded these deliberative speeches as a distinct group. In the summer of 60 he wrote to Atticus:

> As for my little speeches, I'll send both the ones you ask for and some more as well, inasmuch as what I've written down in response to the enthusiasm of young men may also please you. Given that your fellow citizen Demosthenes shone in those speeches which are called the *Philippics*, and that he separated himself from this nit-picking genre of forensic oratory so that he might appear a more lofty statesman, it seemed useful to me to make sure that I too had some speeches which could be called consular.[3]

Cicero then lists for Atticus twelve speeches: four, two very short, on Rullus' agrarian law (three of which survive at least in part); the four Catilinarian speeches; the defence of Rabirius on a charge of *perduellio*; and three speeches of which almost nothing survives, *On Otho*, *On the sons of the proscribed*, and *When I gave up my province in a contio*. There are a number of important points here. One is the distinction between political and forensic speeches, and Cicero's belief that the latter do not add to his reputation in the same way that the former do.[4] Indeed, what we have here is Cicero's recording of the opportunities which holding the consulship gave him to speak in the deliberative genre, opportunities which he had previously had only to a limited extent.[5] Secondly, the reference to Demosthenes is noteworthy: Cicero is self-consciously appropriating the dominant figure in Greek oratory by asserting his mastery in deliberative as well as forensic rhetoric. And there is also the presentation of his work as a specific and deliberate body of work, his 'consular speeches'. For all the deprecatory style of the passage – the clustering of diminutives, the disingenuous explanation that he has written them down because young men want them – we should read this as a testing out, in front of a sympathetic but not uncritical reader, of one particular record of Cicero's consulship.

A problem remains, however, and that is the date: this letter was sent in June 60. Why has Cicero delayed for two and a half years? And, given the delay, must we not accept at face value his statement here that he has produced written versions because of the 'enthusiasm of young men'; that is, that this delayed publication is evidence that Cicero published his speeches for pedagogical and not political ends?[6] For, if his motives primarily connected with his self-presentation, why was publication of these speeches not immediate?

Two sets of considerations suggest that the delay need not demonstrate that Cicero is concerned only about teaching. One is the context of these remarks on the speeches; the other is the political situation in Rome. In this letter to Atticus, Cicero talks about literary activities other than these speeches, and in fact he is picking up on matters that are mentioned in earlier letters. In March of 60, he refers to a Greek account of his consulship which he has sent to Atticus, and promises that if he also writes one in Latin he will send that too. He also tells Atticus to expect a third item, a poem, 'so as not to leave any form of self-praise untried'; and concludes the paragraph by defending himself against an imagined charge from Atticus of self-praise: there is nothing more worth praising, and anyway his works are historical rather than encomia.[7] In the next surviving letter, a little more than two months later, he notes that he has sent the Greek account of his consulship to Atticus a second time, by a different bearer. He then says, 'If others write, I'll send theirs to you; but believe me, once they read mine, for some reason or other they back off.'[8] And then the letter containing the list of 'consular' speeches starts with a reference to *Atticus*' account of Cicero's consulship in Greek which he has just received. He congratulates himself on the fact that, having already dispatched his own piece, he could not be accused of plagiarism; he then compares the two pieces, setting Atticus' plainness against his own highly ornate and carefully prepared style. He returns to a matter he mentioned in the previous letter: the possibility that someone else might use his sketch as the basis for another work. Posidonius has already written: as soon as he read Cicero's piece, he was deterred from writing on the same subject.[9] Cicero draws a positive conclusion from this: 'the horde of people who were pressing me to provide something they could dress up have now stopped pestering me'. He concludes the subject by asking Atticus to see to the distribution of his account, and with the confident hope that it will add something to his reputation.

Cicero's corpus of consular orations is, then, introduced at a point when he is concerned across the board with the written record of his consulship, and is considering, and indeed producing, works in other genres: poetry, prose summaries and more elaborate pieces of historiography proper on the basis of his notes; and when he is conscious that Atticus might think of reproaching him with excessive self-praise. It would make sense to view the speeches as part of this carefully orchestrated management of the recording of Cicero's consulship – an interpretation strengthened by the acute generic sensitivity of the passage and its dialogue with literary history and, specifically, Greek oratorical models. But it need not be the case that this is the first time that the written versions have been disseminated.[10] It is possible that original publication did follow delivery quite swiftly, and that what Cicero is here describing is an act of editing, whereby previously published work is gathered together to form a unified record of his consular oratory. It is also worth noting that Cicero envisaged a situation in which he was not the only person to write about his consulship: but that he was having difficulty in enlisting others. This is an issue that will recur.

It remains to ask why there is a burst of interest during 60. It could be argued that, to a certain extent, this is an illusion, generated by the scarcity of earlier letters to Atticus. In particular, there are none during 62; but it is clear from the three speeches given this year, of which he had versions disseminated, that he was already concerned both with how other people viewed his consulship and with the desire to have it recorded in poetic form. In *On behalf of Sulla* the Catilinarian dimension is impossible to avoid, since Sulla was being tried on charges of violence relating to his alleged involvement in the conspiracy. But Cicero's own position is at the forefront in two early digressions in the speech. In the first (2-10) he justifies his decision to defend a man accused of participating in the conspiracy which he suppressed; in the second (21-35) he defends himself against Torquatus' accusation that he exercised tyrannical domination. He apologises at the start of the first digression for talking about himself: 'I would not use this kind of speech at this point, gentlemen of the jury, if it were simply a matter of my own position: I have many opportunities to speak of my own laudable achievements, and will continue to have them.'[11] But he explains that Torquatus' attack has damaged his authority and hence must be dealt with if he is to defend his client properly. During this digression, he denies that he is cruel (7-8); the demands of the state forced him for a while to be stern, but even that is in conflict with his innate instincts. In the second digression he responds to Torquatus' saying that Cicero's tyranny is unendurable.[12]

In this speech Cicero is responding to Torquatus' speech, and thus most of his self-presentation is defensive and arguing for negatives: he is *not* cruel, he is *not* tyrannical (although he does deliver an impassioned positive defence of his achievements in §33). Elsewhere, he has more freedom to shape his image. In *On behalf of Archias*, the defence of a poet who was accused of falsely claiming to be a Roman citizen, Cicero deals with the factual issues fairly quickly and concentrates on the value of the poet as recorder of great deeds, since the prospect of an undying memory is an incentive to do those things which will deserve to be preserved in poetry. His own hopes that Archias will write about his consulship are offered as an example of this phenomenon (28-30).

The third speech of this year which was disseminated, *Against Quintus Metellus' public meeting*, survives in only a few fragments. Quintus Metellus Nepos had returned to Rome from service in Pompeius' army and stood successfully for the tribunate of 62; he had attacked Cicero's handling of the conspiracy. In Cicero's response, given in the Senate, it seems that he emphasised the Senate's part in events: 'It is your work at issue here, conscript fathers, not mine – and beautiful work it is too, but, as I said, not mine but yours'; 'For it was you who made the decision, you voted, you judged'.[13] From very soon after the events, at least in a senatorial context, Cicero is insisting upon the Senate's responsibility. However, he does so in a manner which also stresses the gap between himself and the Senate as a whole: he and they are distinct entities. Also in 62 he sent a very long letter to Pompeius, then still in the East, describing the achievements of his consulship; at the trial of Sulla, indeed, Torquatus quoted at length from it. Cicero had presumably, therefore, had the text of the letter disseminated at Rome at the same time as it was sent to Pompeius.[14]

It is not, then, a matter of Cicero belatedly realising that he must set the record straight; not only is this in itself implausible but it can be shown to be false from the 62 speeches. How the execution of the conspirators was to be remembered was already a matter for debate; indeed, it was clearly a matter of debate from the very moment Cicero left office.[15] But it is still the case that there is an upsurge in 60; writing the consulship is not an urgent concern in the surviving letters to Atticus from 61. The answer must lie in Cicero's perception of his own circumstances and in particular a sense that he had become more vulnerable.

The letters of this period articulate increasing anxiety about the effectiveness of the Senate and the commitment of various senior figures to its authority, anxieties which crystallise around the trial and acquittal of Publius Clodius on sacrilege charges in the summer of 61. 'That political position, which I thought had been strengthened by divine providence (and you attributed to my direction), which seemed fixed and founded on the unity of all good men and the authority of my consulship, be sure – unless some god takes thought for us – that it has slipped out of our hands by this one verdict.'[16] The following letter laments the increasing estrangement of the equestrian order from the Senate: 'that cobbled together concord' is slipping.[17] This dissolution of the brief, and temporary, unity among disparate groups which had faced the threat of serious violence posed by Catiline is well-documented, as is the way in which Cicero read it as a personal attack, and sought to strengthen his own position by cultivating Pompeius' friendship.[18] What is perhaps less clear is the way that Cicero read this situation as a signal not only to seek support outside the Senate but also to ensure the record of his consulship. Indeed, it is even possible that the rapprochement with Pompeius, whose campaigns in the East were already the subject of laudatory accounts, spurred Cicero on to disseminate his own achievements.

We have already seen that Cicero had difficulty in enlisting any one apart from Atticus to his programme. This continued to be the case. No one wrote a prose work on Cicero's consulship; nor did he get a poem. In the same letter in which he reflects on the disastrous effects of Clodius' acquittal, he also remarks that he must be content with Atticus' epigrams, 'especially since Thyillus has abandoned me and Archias too has written nothing about me – and I'm afraid that since he's finished his Greek poem for the Luculli he's considering a Caecilian drama'.[19] *On behalf of Archias* had not received its hoped-for *quid pro quo*, nor had Thyillus – whose friendship with Cicero is attested back to 67, and who is the author of epigrams in the *Anthology* – written. The historical work too remained unwritten, but Cicero came up with a different solution for the problem of recalcitrant poets. As I discussed in Chapter 1, he wrote an epic about himself, taking over, it seems, the established mechanisms of epic, including a third-person narrator, to write autobiography.

The poem, which appears to be what Cicero is referring to in *Att.* 1.19, was completed by December of 60, since he quotes three lines from the third book in a letter to Atticus from that month.[20] The context is an approach from Balbus, an associate of Caesar, asking Cicero to co-operate with Caesar during his consulship: having listed the advantages that this course of action would bring him, Cicero exhorts himself to refuse by means of his own poetry. The way that the lines are quoted suggests that this is not their unveiling: 'So Calliope herself instructed me in that book in which there are many aristocratic views.'[21] The implication is that Atticus has access to a copy, but may be still unfamiliar enough with the work to need a reminder about details; and as Atticus had been back in Rome since late summer of 60 (and there are no letters between June and December) he was presumably given a copy as soon as it was completed. Once Cicero had decided to write on his own behalf, he did not waste time.

Although over eighty lines survive, almost all come from a single, long quotation in *On divination* from a speech by the muse Urania, and it is not entirely certain in what order the remaining fragments fitted into the three-book structure,[22] though parts seem to have given scope to Cicero's oratorical skills: two or three lines appear to come from an invective against the conspirators. The poem seems to have taken a staunchly optimate line: quite apart from Cicero's own description of it as written 'aristocratically', the long passage from *On divination* is not only an extended affirmation of the validity of Roman divinatory practice but locates it also in an extended Roman past: 'Rightly, therefore, did your ancestors … worship most attentively the ever-flourishing gods' (lines 66-70). Moreover, the threat that Catiline poses is primarily, in Urania's telling, to order: 'the death of laws' (line 51), the destruction of the city and of the temples of the gods were all portended.

In addition, however, Cicero places intellectual activity in the forefront of his treatment. This long quotation concludes with the lines: 'So they who in happiness passed their leisure in distinguished studies saw deeply these things with prudent care, and in the shady Academy and shining Lyceum poured out the fine skill of fruitful hearts. Your country placed you, summoned from these in the first flower of your youth, in the midst of virtue's struggle. And yet you soothe anxious cares with rest and dedicate to learning and to us what is left free from your country's service.' The passage thus places Roman religion within a Greek philosophical context. This context has already been apparent in the opening words of Urania's speech, in which a Stoic view of the universe is expounded as a philosophical justification for divination – indeed, this is why Cicero has his brother Quintus quote the passage in *On divination*. In the closing words, however, divination does not merely receive philosophical support, but the archetypically Roman and historically grounded act of religious practice has become the property of those who study in Athens. With the sort of imperceptible shift so familiar from his oratory, Cicero is inserting Greek philosophy into the religious knowledge of the Roman élite.

Against this general background, Cicero develops two further personal claims. One is that his own intellectual activities are justified. Urania picks him out specifically as one who has been called back from his studies at Athens to serve his country, and reminds the reader that these studies are invariably subordinated to the needs of Rome. Cicero's intellectual interests thus become central to his ability to protect Rome, both through the link between philosophy and divination and, in these final lines, with the suggestion that their capacity to alleviate mental distress has helped Cicero do what must be done.[23] (At the same time Cicero is associated with the figures of the past who understood the importance of divine worship.) It may even be that a reader can understand line 74, 'they poured out the fine skill of fruitful hearts', as a reference not simply to philosophical speech but also to rhetoric. Finally, it is arguable that the passage as a whole refers to Cicero's other poetry. When Urania says (lines 6-7), 'and if you wish to know the movements and the wandering tracks of the stars', the main clause is the statement, 'you may see them now all marked out by the divine mind' and this refers to Jupiter. But a reader might initially think that the reference was to Cicero's own description of the stars in his translation of Aratus. Moreover, *diuinus* is already used in poetry to describe the prophetic utterance of mortals: Ennius used it of Anchises (fr. 15-16 Skutsch). Within a few years both Catullus and Lucretius would apply it to poetry.[24] It is at least possible that the misreading of lines 6-7 continues throughout this sentence and that the *diuina mens* can be taken, at least on first sight, in relation to Cicero's divinely inspired activities as the translator of Aratus.[25] Urania then states that Cicero surveyed 'the swift movements of the stars and the serious conjunctions of the stars with flashing light' as consul: at the very least, the alert reader could reflect that Cicero was in an excellent position to understand what he saw.

I would suggest, therefore, that Cicero's handling of his consulship in verse draws self-consciously on his identity as a poet; and does not simply cross-refer to his earlier work but presents it as an integral part of his activities as a statesman. As far as *His consulship* is concerned, Cicero was able to suppress the Catilinarian conspiracy because of the sort of person he was; and part of his identity was that of an intellectual and a poet. This work marks an integration of the different strands in Cicero's identity.

Although the fragmentary state of the poem as a whole makes further comment uncertain, two aspects of it can be asserted with some confidence. One was the importance of Cicero's role in it, as I discussed in Chapter 1: he was the saviour of the state, responsible for its rebirth. The other was the stress on peace and on Cicero's position as a civilian leader. These two aspects are summed up in the two best-known lines of the poem: *o fortunatam natam me consule Romam* (Fortunate Rome, born in my consulship) and *cedant arma togae, concedat laurea laudi* (Let arms yield to the toga, let the laurels give way to praise). These lines are well known and frequently quoted: only five hexameters survive from *His consulship* which are not quoted by Cicero, and the other three lines depend on single citations in Nonius and [Probus]: this pair were the only ones to enter the common language of quotation.[26] And it is clear that they made a huge impact, though this cannot be traced until after Cicero returned from exile. But before considering his post-exile position, it is worth considering their content a little more closely.

O fortunatam natam me consule Romam is a direct reference to one of the honorific gestures in the aftermath of the conspiracy. Cicero was hailed by Catulus, in the Senate, as *pater patriae*.[27] Parents give birth: this line takes to a logical conclusion what was implicit in the phrase.[28] Cicero is not simply, therefore, engaging in a piece of tasteful self-aggrandisement; he is attempting to make a permanent record of a laudatory gesture which others made towards him. Similarly, the line about arms yielding to togas enshrines another important aspect of Cicero's actions: that he had dealt successfully with a threat which was in Rome itself and had done so without bloodshed in the city. This line could also, however, be read as a comment on the relationship between Cicero and Pompeius: Pompeius, the greatest general of the day, eclipsed by a civilian. Others certainly read the line in that way: and Cicero's denials, after his return from exile, are vehement. But what was the situation in 60?

A key document here would be the lost letter from Cicero to Pompeius describing the achievements of the year. Pompeius appears not to have been pleased with its tone, which is described by a scholiast on Cicero's speeches as 'rather arrogant'. He failed to congratulate Cicero on what he had accomplished when he replied; that at least is the implication of a short letter from Cicero to Pompeius, which does survive, from April 62. In it, Cicero replies both to an open letter from Pompeius and to one which he sent to Cicero personally; he assures Pompeius of the delight with which the public letter was generally received and complains that he himself received no thanks in Pompeius' personal letter.[29]

There is no indication that Cicero himself intended *Fam.* 5.7 for an audience other than Pompeius, but he could not of course determine what Pompeius would do with it. And to a certain extent the distinction between public and private need not be drawn firmly here: not simply because the boundaries were permeable but because this is an absolutely formal and public piece of writing, regardless of how many people in fact read it. Cicero is continuing his negotiations with Pompeius and the subject is the state and the roles which Pompeius and Cicero may, together, play in its management. Cicero expounds a linked series of ideas. Pompeius' grudging response to what Cicero has accomplished is not an insuperable barrier to their co-operation; nonetheless, it has been noted, and consequently Pompeius is still obliged to Cicero for his actions. But Cicero provides an excuse for Pompeius' omission: 'I think you omitted it because you were afraid of offending anyone.'[30] Finally, he assures Pompeius that his actions have met with universal approval, and when Pompeius returns he too will understand this and accept Cicero's friendship, as a Laelius to his Africanus.

In the reading of these exchanges, the notion of a blindly boasting Cicero is not particularly helpful. Cicero was unlikely to have been surprised by Pompeius' unenthusiastic response to his initial long account: from the end of December 63 Metellus Nepos, who had just taken up his position as one of the tribunes of 62, had been attempting to undermine Cicero's position and he was closely connected with Pompeius, both through marriage and as a former legate who had returned from service with Pompeius' army in the East to stand for election. This is not to say that he was acting on Pompeius' instructions: the difficulty and slowness of communication would preclude any detailed guidance, and Pompeius was eventually unimpressed by Nepos' clumsy attempts to have him recalled.[31] But although Cicero may not have identified Nepos with Pompeius, it would nonetheless have been the case that Nepos' actions could more generally be interpreted as a sign of Pompeius' hostility towards him. And if this is the case, then Cicero's long public letter to Pompeius is a reaction to circumstances. In it he attempts to persuade Pompeius that he is wrong by a demonstration of the strength of his achievement, and thus that he is in a position to offer Pompeius useful support. A display of humility would have achieved nothing. And Pompeius' response was a response not to the tone of Cicero's letter, but in accordance with his perception of what the real situation was. That is, Cicero failed to gain his ends immediately not because he was an inept manipulator of language but because even he could not convince Pompeius of the magnitude of what he had done. Hence, indeed, his reference in his second attempt, the surviving *Fam.* 5.7, to the transformation in Pompeius' understanding that will happen once he has returned to Italy. Cicero is attempting in this letter to trump written accounts with an appeal to autopsy.

This letter also demonstrates that Cicero's proposed co-operation with Pompeius is based on a clear demarcation of spheres. When he sets himself up as a Laelius to Pompeius' Africanus, he is claiming civilian authority to complement Pompeius' military success. And this is the interpretation he insists upon throughout *On his consulship* two years later. Cicero constructs his authority in the aftermath of the Catilinarian conspiracy in such a way that it leaves room for Pompeius, even though he is also attempting to undermine the inevitable superiority of arms. *Cedant arma togae* failed, but to concentrate on the failure at the expense of understanding what the aim was is a mistake. Cicero was trying to make up the huge shortfall he faced in reputation because of his lack of military achievements: the fragments of the *On his consulship* which survive indicate that he did so by appealing to the city of Rome. Its salvation was both Cicero's own and a uniquely civilian achievement: Rome was, of course, an entirely demilitarised area and *could* only be saved by a togate protector.

Elements in Cicero's portrayal of self fit into a possible framework for co-operation with Pompeius. But the Pompeius towards whom Cicero is reacting is himself to an extent a textual creation. This was in part because Pompeius had not been in Rome since 67 BC: how he was perceived was inevitably filtered through the reports of others and his own letters. But he had also succeeded in getting others to memorialise him. Theophanes of Mytilene had a quasi-official place in his army, wrote an account of Pompeius' campaigns, and became a Roman on the strength of this.[32] Posidonius was eventually to write on Pompeius.[33] Cicero was not doing anything odd in seeking to record himself; what was different was that he relied on his own efforts to do it.

Cicero presents himself in the period between his consulship and his departure into exile in the spring of 58 as the heroic civilian defender of the Roman state, whose suppression of the Catilinarian conspiracy is both the pinnacle of his own career and a moment of enormous peril to the state which was nonetheless successfully withstood through the actions of a single individual. He transmits this message in a variety of media: the speeches which he delivered during the year, an epic poem, a prose summary in Greek and possibly one in Latin, and a semi-public letter. Insofar as we can determine from the surviving works, the nuances of the presentation vary according to the type of work but the broad lines remain the same: peril to the state averted through the vigilance of a single civilian. It is worth drawing attention also to the fact that Cicero frequently appears as a solitary figure in these works. He is acting on his own. This is particularly apparent in the *Catilinarians*: although he refers to the support he has from elements within the state, the actual process of decision-making is his alone.[34] Indeed, towards the end of the first *Catilinarian* he draws attention to the lack of support he has from the Senate:

> There are some members of this order who either do not see what is coming or pretend that what they see does not exist; who nourish Catiline's hopes by their flabby views and strengthen the growing conspiracy by not believing in it; and if I were to punish Catiline their influence would lead many – the naïve as well as criminals – to say that I had acted cruelly and tyrannically.[35]

To a certain extent Cicero is making the best of the fact that he did not have the backing of the entire Senate during this period, though this presentation also has dramatic force in pitting a solitary and wakeful consul against the forces which menace Rome. The speech *Against Quintus Metellus' public meeting* seems to have attempted to place the responsibility with the Senate, as Cicero faced an immediate challenge to what he had had done; but he himself is a figure distinct from the Senate.

As a means of protecting himself, these textual presences did not succeed; Cicero was unable to maintain his position sufficiently to defend himself against the charge that he had put citizens to death without trial. Publius Clodius, an enemy of Cicero from the date of the Bona Dea trial in 61, was able in 59, with the assistance of Julius Caesar, to shed his patrician status through adoption and therefore stand for election to the tribunate; and once tribune, in 58, he promulgated legislation exiling those who had executed citizens without trial.[36] Cicero did not wait for legal proceedings but departed from Italy, settling eventually in Thessalonica, where he spent a wretched year until Clodius' measure could be successfully challenged by his friends. Cicero returned to Rome in apparent triumph in September 57 and immediately set about rebuilding his public image through a range of speeches. But the nature of his self-presentation has rather different emphases from those apparent in the works written between consulship and exile.

The 50s

Cicero was busy as an orator in the five years or so between his return from exile and his departure to become governor of Cilicia, and many of his speeches arose from the circumstances of his exile and return. Immediately on his return he thanked the Senate and the people; shortly afterwards he spoke in front of the college of pontifices challenging the dedication of the site of his house by Clodius (*On his house*); and he also disseminated the text of a speech he delivered in a senatorial debate on the soothsayers' interpretation of an earthquake near Rome, *On the replies of the soothsayers*. Moreover, he took and created opportunities to attack those whom he held responsible for his exile, namely, in addition to Clodius, the consuls of 58 Piso and Gabinius: he attacked the two consuls in his speech *On the consular provinces* and delivered an invective specifically against Piso, *Against Piso*; and there are passages of invective in other speeches. Clodius' wrong-doing was clear; Piso and Gabinius are singled out because they did not stop Clodius from attacking Cicero, although their position as consuls meant they could have taken action had they chosen.

This oratorical activity, and the accompanying dissemination of texts, can be seen as an attempt by Cicero to regain the standing and influence he had lost at the point, in March 58, when he had decided to resist Clodius no further and anticipate his legislative threats by leaving Italy. It is a programme of reconstruction within careful limits: Cicero identifies Piso and Gabinius as the men who have wronged him. He does not point the finger at Pompeius or Caesar, whose decisions had ultimately set up the circumstances for Cicero's exile, Pompeius by withdrawing his support in the spring of 58, Caesar by acquiescing the previous year in Clodius' shedding of his patrician status, an essential precondition for standing for the tribunate. And he is extremely circumspect in his attacks on Clodius, and in particular is very cautious about naming Clodius. Cicero's programme of self-reconstruction is, therefore, realistic: he was not in a position to challenge either Pompeius or Caesar, and Clodius himself needed handling with great care; but the consuls of 58, now absent from Rome in their provinces, were feasible targets and attacking them was an attempt by Cicero to demonstrate that he had regained his position.

Among these speeches *On the replies of the soothsayers* is particularly suggestive for the question of Cicero's self-presentation, since it is an attempt to fix the historical record on a particular issue in his favour and against Clodius. The soothsayers, when consulted about the earthquake and various other portents in 56, had pronounced them due to a variety of human transgressions, including the occupation of holy places.[37] Clodius had claimed in the Senate that this referred to Cicero's rebuilding of his house, on a site which Clodius had consecrated to Freedom during Cicero's absence; Cicero's speech is a rebuttal of this claim and an argument that the soothsayers' report refers to things which Clodius has done.

An important element in how Cicero does this is his claim that others support him. In responding to Clodius' claim that the rebuilding of his house is the cause of the problem he emphasises that Clodius' consecration of the site was completely invalid:

> In the first place my enemy himself, in that dark stormy night of the State, ... never touched my house with a single letter of sanctity; then, the Roman people, whose authority over all matters is supreme, ordered, in a meeting of the *comitia centuriata* by the votes of all ages and classes, that that house should have the same status that it had had previously; and finally you, Conscript Fathers, decreed that the question of the sanctity of my house should be referred to the college of pontifices – not because there was any doubt in the matter, but in order to silence this fury, should he remain longer in the city which he wished to destroy.[38]

Cicero thus draws attention to the technical invalidity of Clodius' dedication, but more important in the list are the consensus of people and Senate. This consensus is then crowned by the unanimous decision of the pontifices in his favour (12) and Cicero emphasises both the solemnity and unanimity of this decision by listing the names of the nineteen priests involved.

This strategy is an effective counter to Clodius' argument: Cicero's house cannot be the place which the soothsayers were referring to, since its lack of sanctity has been guaranteed by people, Senate and pontifices. But this emphasis on the range of support and of decisions in favour of Cicero also underscores his reintegration into Roman society. He has everybody's backing, except that of Clodius. And he draws on this extended support also in his opening attack on Clodius. Having described how Clodius collapsed in the face of a Ciceronian onslaught in the Senate the previous day he draws breath, as it were, and continues:

> What shall I say about his unbridled and headlong madness? Or can he be wounded by words from me stronger than those with which he was overwhelmed and butchered in the very deed by that most distinguished man Publius Servilius? And even if I could match his unique and almost divine forcefulness and authority I do not doubt the weapons which his enemy throws seem lighter and blunter than those which his father's colleague [sc. P. Servilius Isauricus] dispatched.[39]

Cicero comes close to admitting that his assaults on Clodius are vitiated by his known enmity; but this allows him to harness the authority of Servilius to his cause. Servilius, who had been consul in 79, was in his late seventies and probably the eldest active consular; his enormously distinguished career included two triumphs and the acquisition of an honorific cognomen, Isauricus, from his campaign against the pirates; and his words against Clodius the previous day gained further force from the fact of Clodius' father having been his consular colleague (and possibly too from the relationship between the two men).[40]

Cicero thus builds into his interpretation the sense of a community which is supporting him. But he is concerned not simply with their support for him but also with their unity among themselves more generally. The concluding part of the speech offers a pessimistic assessment of the position of the state and an appeal to unity as the only possible hope:

> Once our state was so strong and robust that it could withstand the bypassing of the Senate and even acts of aggression against individual citizens. It can no longer do so. The treasury is empty, those who have undertaken public contracts are making no profit from them, the authority of the leading men has collapsed, the agreement between classes has been torn apart, the courts have failed, voting tablets are controlled by a few, the support of good men will soon no longer be at the disposal of our order, and you will look in vain for a citizen who will suffer hatred for the sake of his country's safety. Since this is the current position, we can survive only through unity; ....[41]

Unity, *concordia*, is the only possible way forward. And in the final words of the speech Cicero sets up an antithesis between prayers, which are straightforward now that the soothsayers have spoken, and the task of his audience, which is 'to resolve the anger and disputes which exist between us'. Cicero is not undermining the authority and importance of religious observance, but he is using the discussion of religious affairs to emphasise that there are problems which the Senate itself must solve.

Cicero is thus in this speech attempting to place himself within a united commonwealth. But he is not claiming an outstandingly prominent part within this coalition. We have already seen how he yields to Servilius Isauricus in the opening paragraphs of the speech; and towards the end he says,

> I would not have undertaken such a serious and gloomy speech, conscript fathers – not because I could not or did not have an obligation to maintain this role and activity, given the offices which the Roman people have bestowed upon me and the many honours I have received from you – but it would have been easy to stay silent when others were silent; but the whole of this speech is concerned not with my standing but with the state religion.[42]

Cicero denies personal ambition in delivering this speech, while reminding his audience of his eminence; but he also treats his position and the obligations it entails as due to the support of the people and Senate and not to any achievement of his own. He is speaking in order to preserve the state by ensuring that its religious duties are carried out properly, and not to bolster his own position; hence, he implies, the attacks on Clodius and on Piso and Gabinius are justified because their actions are threats to the state; their dealings with Cicero are relevant only insofar as they are manifestations of a threat to the state.

This stance is somewhat different in emphasis from that which Cicero was projecting between his consulship and exile. There, the stress was on his achievement and his solitude; here, upon identifying Clodius' attack on him with a more general attack on the state. The Catilinarian conspiracy has receded; Cicero claims attention now because he is resisting a figure whom he claims is a threat to all. One could argue, indeed, that Clodius has replaced Catiline and that Cicero is still, fundamentally, defining himself against a common enemy; but he now stresses more firmly that he does so as part of a wider coalition of right-thinking men rather than as a peculiarly privileged individual.

There is, however, one respect in which Cicero's self-presentation in *On the soothsayers' replies*, at least, picks up on his persona immediately after his consulship, and that is as a man of letters. In §§18-19 Cicero claims the authority to speak on religious matters because his studies have reinforced his conviction that the gods exist and protect the Roman state. He starts with a reassurance: 'Even if I might seem to have spent more time in the study of literature than other men who are equally busy, nonetheless I am not someone who derives any pleasure from writings which deter and distract our minds from religion.'[43] He then claims two types of engagement with religion. One is the respect he pays to ancestral religion; the other, 'insofar as I have any leisure, I have learnt that many wise and learned men have spoken and left writings about the spirit of the immortal gods; and however divinely inspired these writings seem to be, nonetheless they are of such a kind that our ancestors seem to have taught the authors and not be taught by them'.[44] So Cicero is

67

arguing that his philosophical studies not only do not undermine his respect and attachment to Roman religion but in fact are in complete accord with the practice of religion.

Cicero is notably unspecific about details here. The 'writings which deter and distract our minds from religion' may be Epicurean, at this point probably the only philosophical treatises in Latin; and the suggestion that earlier generations at Rome did not learn their religious practices from others is an oblique correction of the belief, which was current at least by the early second century, that Numa, the second king of Rome who traditionally established religious behaviour, was an adherent of Pythagoras.[45] That is, these remarks do not spring from a vacuum; but it remains to ask why Cicero raises the subject in this speech. It is possible that Clodius had attacked him in these terms during the struggle over the site of Cicero's house; but even if that is the case, Cicero is responding by embracing his intellectual reputation and demonstrating that it coheres with traditional practice. As in *His consulship*, Cicero's public actions are intimately linked with his private studies.

At the same time that Cicero is projecting this altered self, the way that he had presented himself after the Catilinarian conspiracy provided rich material for those who wished to attack him. In *On his house* he records that Clodius has told him to stop boasting, and said that it is unbearable that Cicero calls himself Jupiter, and says that Minerva is his sister (92). This claim does not appear in any of Cicero's surviving works: its most probable location is in *His consulship*. And in *Against Piso*, a response to an attack in the Senate on him by Piso (itself replying to Cicero's attacks on him in the period since he, Cicero, had returned from exile) which he delivered in 55, he has to deal with Piso's criticisms of his poetry: ' "Envy didn't harm you, but your poetry" ' (72) which, on Cicero's telling, centred on the line, 'Let arms yield to the toga, let laurels yield to praise'. In the *Invective against Cicero*, of unknown date, an attack on his poetry, centred around that line and 'Fortunate Rome, born when I was consul', occupies about a quarter of the whole work: 'I beg you, Cicero, you can have done and accomplished whatever you like, it is enough that we have endured it; do you also load our ears with your offensiveness and pursue us with infuriating words?' (6).[46] It is notable that all this invective about Cicero's writings centres on his poetry; his other works do not feature. Why should this be the case? By the first century AD his poetry is criticised because it was regarded as poor in quality.[47] But the nature of the criticism that Cicero seems to be responding to, and that which is found in the *Invective against Cicero*, does not suggest that the attack was on aesthetic grounds alone. Rather, Cicero's claims about the nature of his achievement, in particular his association with the gods and his setting himself up as the saviour of the state whose actions are more valuable than those of military commanders, provoke animosity. This is a matter of content as well as style.

Arguably, the poetry is singled out because of the novelty of the form. It was precisely the fact that writing epic poetry about oneself allowed one artistic control that also made it potentially offensive: the gap between the man praised and the man praising had collapsed, and praise become self-praise. Cicero's generic inventiveness provoked a response. And Cicero does not accept the criticisms. In *On his house* and *Against Piso* he counterattacks vigorously; and towards the end of *On his house*, Jupiter and Minerva, 'who has always been my helper in my plans', head the list of those invoked as witnesses to his self-devotion, the requital for which is the restoration of his house (144-5). It is tempting to see this as a defiant gesture towards Clodius' criticism.[48]

In the aftermath of his consulship Cicero tried out a large number of types of writing as means of transmitting himself, and emphasised particularly that he was the solitary civilian defender of the state from the menace of Catiline. Once he returned from exile, we can see him defending this presentation and particularly its manifestation in poetry from explicit attack, while in general recasting himself to face changed circumstances: the enmity of Clodius and the lack of support that had led to his having to go into exile. Cicero tried out one public persona; when it demonstrably did not command widespread support, he modified it to one which might.

The invention of the politician

In the second half of the 50s Cicero put his intellectual interests to the more direct service of the state with a trilogy of rhetorical and philosophical works, *On the orator*, *On the state* and *On the laws*. Whereas his earlier works, with the exception perhaps of his poetic juvenilia, had all been concerned with 'Cicero', the prose treatises of the 50s consider a concept of the public figure which is, at least on the surface, not a direct portrait of Cicero himself.

In *On the orator* and *On the state* Cicero is engaged in the apparent creation of a new category within Roman political thought, that of the 'politician' or 'statesman'. This figure is a man who is constantly engaged in civilian activity for the good of the state. Hence it marks a departure from the established pattern of the *cursus honorum*, which involved the regular alternation of activity as a magistrate with periods in which no public office was held. Arguably, Cicero is attempting to create a civilian counterpart to the military commanders whose terms of office now increasingly extended over several years and as a result now not of annual prorogation by the Senate but through laws which determined in advance the length of *imperium*. We have already seen that the relationship which Cicero attempted to establish between himself and Pompeius in the aftermath of the Catilinarian conspiracy relied upon a distinction between civilian and military spheres of operation, and indeed that Cicero's self-presentation as a consul emphasised his togate credentials: in the late 50s he generalises his experience in order to present a category of activity which is both new and, on Cicero's telling, essential.

The subject of *On the orator* is, ostensibly, the orator: that is, the man who speaks well.[49] Cicero presents it in the opening chapters as a replacement for his *On invention*: the implication is that oratory cannot be dealt with simply through a technical handbook but is an activity whose nature, purpose and achievement can only be handled discursively by those who have successfully engaged in it. Moreover, the orator must be at home in disciplines other than oratory. In all this it is clear that, despite the dialogue's setting in the past, Cicero is portraying a conception of the orator which he himself – but perhaps not others – does match.

The idea of the politician is introduced to the work obliquely. After the opening frame, book 1 contains a discussion of eloquence and then Crassus, one of the work's two chief characters (the other is Antonius) discusses the need for training and for a knowledge of the law. Then, over two-thirds of the way through the first book, Crassus asks Antonius to respond to his exposition. Antonius starts his response with the claim that they must determine what their conversation is actually about. In order to do this, they need to look at practitioners. He explains what he means by a series of examples: if one wanted to know what the art of the general was, one would look at what generals did, and he then names some famous generals. He then lists a number of other activities: being a legal expert, a musician, a teacher of language, a poet or a philosopher. But the second example in his list is different. 'If we were asking who that man was who brought his experience and knowledge and commitment to guiding the state, I would define him in this way: the man who understands and uses the means whereby the benefit of the state is served and increased should be considered as the regulator of the state and the author of public policy'.[50] Antonius then specifies five Romans by name whom he thinks fit these criteria.

This second example offers a curiously anomalous argument. In every other case, there is a clearly defined individual, such as a general, or a poet, or a philosopher, whose activities as a general or poet or philosophy can be used a basis to determine what generalship, or poetry, or philosophy actually *is*. But with the second example Antonius does not have a neat title for an activity. Rather, he indicates the man he is talking about through a description of what he does. So an individual is denoted by a relative clause describing what he does, and he is then defined by another relative clause describing what he does (in different terms).

Moreover, there was no need for Antonius to use this example at all. The other cases on his list are more than adequate by themselves to indicate his method: look at the practitioner and that will tell you what the art is. This second case merely disrupts the flow of the argument, and it is tempting to see the irruption of this apparently

71

disruptive example as an indication of one of the deeper concerns of the work: the nature of the man in public life. Antonius gives five examples of men he judges to be in this category: Publius Cornelius Lentulus, Tiberius Gracchus the elder, Quintus Caecilius Metellus (Macedonicus), Publius Cornelius Scipio Aemilianus and Gaius Laelius. Judging by these, what Antonius has in mind is not simply outstanding eminence, though all five held the consulship: rather it is a combination of longevity and political soundness. Scipio Aemilianus was the most famous and militarily the most noted: he would emerge as the central figure in *On the state*, written immediately after *On the orator*, together with Gaius Laelius as his close friend, ally, and confidant. It is not perhaps surprising that Cicero should already view him as a political hero. The claims of the other three need further unravelling.

The Publius Lentulus in the list is the man who was *princeps senatus*, 'leader of the Senate', between 125 and his death some time after 120; but at the time of his appointment to the position by the censors of 125 he must have been nearly eighty, since he held the (suffect) consulship in 162. He was notorious as one of the senior figures who responded to the call of the consul Opimius in 121 and participated in the defeat of Gaius Gracchus, and subsequently left Rome for Sicily due to the hatred his conduct had aroused.[51] Tiberius Gracchus was the father of the tribunes; he has already been named in *On the orator* (1.38) by Scaevola (who is arguing that eloquence is not a benefit to communities) as an example of a man who was not eloquent but who did good to the state through the exercise of his authority and wisdom. And Quintus Metellus, the consul of 143, had two claims to lasting fame: as censor he urged the necessity of this institution of marriage; and he was the father of four sons, all of whom reached the consulship. Cicero has gathered together a group of men who demonstrate sustained commitment, at the highest level, to the good of the Roman state over an extended period of years.

Antonius proceeds to insist that oratory and statesmanship are not the same, and that those who are prominent in the management of the state's affairs gain their results through their standing, their judgement and their wisdom.[52] Oratory belongs rather to legal activity. A constant difficulty in the interpretation of Cicero's treatises in dialogue form is the extent to which any character can be deemed to be articulating Cicero's own views: and while the debate in *On the orator* is more a matter of form than genuine and substantial differences of belief, it is Crassus, of the two main interlocutors, who seems to be closer to Cicero. On the wider topic at stake in this passage, whether the orator must have a wide general education, Antonius, who denies that this is the case, is supporting the position which Cicero identified at the opening of the work as contrary to his own (1.5). We should be hesitant in accepting Antonius' separation here of statesmanship from oratory without further debate. It is rather that Cicero, through his characters' conversation, is exploring one of the central problems of oratory within a Roman context. Does it contribute to the good of the state? Is it a necessary skill for those who seek to determine policy? These are questions which Scaevola's objection early in the dialogue raised, with the two younger Gracchi as examples of the harmful potential of oratory; and Crassus does not address this objection directly at that stage.[53] Control of oratory remains a problem throughout Cicero's writings on the subject.

How does the concept of the politician help with this dilemma? In *On the orator* Cicero skirts the issue: the work is essentially about the art of rhetoric, in which Cicero takes the well-established five-part division of rhetoric, the basis of textbooks, including his own, and rewrites it as an intellectually challenging and demonstrably effective system of communication. Moreover, he integrates into the five-part system the Aristotelian use of three modes of persuasion, argument, character and emotion, and introduces humour as a key element: an innovation, it seems, in writing on rhetoric, and one which is clearly based in Cicero's own identity and practice as a speaker, however much he is careful to ensure that Caesar Strabo's presentation of the topic is not anachronistic. *On the orator*, then, is primarily concerned to offer a theoretical perspective onto Cicero's practical mastery. But the all-important form of the work means that it is not simply abstract, nor indeed concerned only with Cicero's contribution to oratory. At the simplest level, dialogue form does little to aid the reader's comprehension of *On the orator*: there is too little difference in the positions of Antonius and Crassus, and the device of different speakers is used to break up the exposition rather than to articulate genuinely contrasting perspectives.[54] But the form does enable Cicero to present the serious discussion of oratory, as an art and intellectual discipline, as an occupation of the politically active elite, and thereby reflect upon the place of oratory in public life.

Various factors appear to have influenced Cicero's choice of his seven characters, including credibility and the desire to stretch back into the past. But his major speakers are all men with oratorical abilities. Also, and not perhaps coincidentally, many had not left written speeches behind. As I discussed in the previous chapter, neither Antonius nor Cotta nor Sulpicius had versions of any of their speeches disseminated, and Crassus only 'very few'; Caesar Strabo and Catulus, who did publish some of their speeches, are less important characters in the work. At the very least one could argue that this dearth of written remains helped Cicero to construct an idealising picture of the intellectual achievements of this group. Moreover, we are given a glimpse of oratory in practice in the opening of the third book. Here Cicero describes the speech which Crassus gave in the Senate very shortly after the discussion recorded in *On the orator* and which led directly to his death a few days after that. The context was the breakdown of co-operation between one of the two consuls of 91, Philippus, and the Senate, as the tensions which were to lead to the breakout of the Social war increased, and Crassus' speech was in defence of the authority and integrity of the Senate, and, according to Cicero, of unparalleled brilliance.

Here, then, we might see the working out in practice of the ideal of the orator which the work expresses, in the form of technical skill, understood in its widest sense, being put to use for the benefit of the state. However, the anecdote about Crassus is presented in a noticeably downbeat way. Most obvious is the juxtaposition of Crassus' triumph with his death and indeed the causal connection between the two events: it is while he is delivering the speech that he feels the pain in his side which is the harbinger of the fatal pleurisy (3.6). Moreover, his death comes when he has reached the apex of his career and could have looked forward to exercising his enormous standing with the state. It happens, therefore, at a bitterly inappropriate point: and there are verbal parallels between Cicero's description here of how Crassus' legitimate hopes were foiled and his description of himself at the very beginning of the whole work, a passage which I discuss below.

The sense conveyed that Crassus' death, coming when it did, deprived the Roman state of an enormous talent at its height would, on its own, be a source of pathos, but would not necessarily undermine the role of oratory. But Cicero then goes on to reflect that Crassus was in fact fortunate in the timing of his death, since it spared him from the subsequent horrors of internecine strife at Rome (3.8), and Cicero then considers the fates of five of the other six men involved in the conversation (3.9-11). Four died violently and the fifth, Cotta, was exiled. (Scaevola the augur, who is not mentioned here, probably died of natural causes within a few years of the date of the dialogue.) *On the orator* thus acts as a memorial to an entire generation: I discuss the use of similar mechanisms in later treatises in Chapter 4. Finally, there is little sense that Crassus might have had any effect on subsequent events. His death is indeed a blow to the state (3.8); but, had he lived, the choices which Cicero imagines for him are either death in civil war, or witnessing the death of his country (3.12). Oratory is, it would seem, ineffective is the face of civil strife; indeed, the one member of the group whose later oratory is described in any detail is Sulpicius Rufus, whose speeches as tribune are indicated as an element in the destructive results he achieved (3.11).

On the orator does not give a clear-cut guide to how oratory can best be used in the state's interests; rather, it offers a picture of oratory at work within the Roman state and an emotionally persuasive, albeit logically unsound, link between the deaths of orators and the collapse of the state into chaos. The mutilated nature of *On the state* makes its view of the ideal statesman highly uncertain, but this topic was at least one which the work addressed directly. Cicero describes the first draft, in a letter to his brother, as 'concerned with the best form of government and with the best citizen' and this remained the work's focus, despite changes to the original plan for the structure.[55] Book 1 dealt with constitutions, book 2 related Rome's history to a constitutional framework and book 3 contained a debate on the possibility of states being just. Book 4 seems to have dealt with the education of citizens, book 5 the nature of the *rector rei publicae* and book 6, which concluded with the surviving Dream of Scipio, how the statesman must act at times of crisis. Cicero's summary for Quintus uses the word *ciuis*, citizen, which sidesteps the problem evident in *On the orator,* of how to describe the politician; but in the final two books of *On the state*, in which Cicero was concerned not with the citizen body as a whole but with the out-standing politician, this issue re-emerges. His solution seems to have been the phrase *rector rei publicae*; the same phrase which was used by Antonius to denote his politically engaged man in *On the orator.*

The nature of the *rector rei publicae* was the focus of enormous scholarly discussion in the last century: many understood Cicero here to be adumbrating a specific, and constitutionally established, office with the Roman state and thus re-introducing a monarchical element into the constitution. This is, however, a misapprehension: Cicero is discussing a type of individual, and not an office.[56] Indeed, the separation of this concept from the mechanics of office-holding is important, since Cicero is exploring the nature of the individual whose involvement in the running of the state is continuous. The fragments of book 5 indicate some aspects of the *rector*: he will manifest traditional morality (fr. 1); he will be knowledgeable about the law, but will not distract himself by practising it (fr. 5); he will inculcate shame among the citizens (fr. 6); and the ends toward which he is striving are summed up as 'the happy existence of the citizens, so that it may be secure in resources, rich in property, substantial in renown and honourable in its virtue' (fr. 8a).[57] There was also some discussion of the necessity, or otherwise, of the statesman's knowing oratory; and the fragments which seem to address this issue (fr. 11b, 11c) are also reminders that much of this book seems to have consisted of exposition by Scipio Aemilianus, and cannot therefore be treated as expressions of Cicero's own views: certainly, what Cicero has Scipio say about parallels between bribery and oratory (11b) is unlikely to correspond exactly with his own beliefs. *On the state* is not a straightforward exposition: show-ing Roman aristocrats in the act of discussing contested issues is central to Cicero's project of placing intellectual debate at the heart of public life.

2. Cicero as a Public Figure

Most of book 6 is also fragmentary: what survives indicates that the first part of the book included a discussion by Scipio of the behaviour which the statesman needed to display at times of dissension and crisis. But his discussion concludes with the exposition of the rewards which await the statesman after his death.[58] Scipio expounds a dream which he had as a young officer in North Africa during the third Punic war : after a meeting with Massinissa, the king of Numidia, he dreamt that his (adoptive) grandfather Scipio Africanus appeared to him and explained that there is a posthumous existence in the heavens for the virtuous. The episode is parallel to the Myth of Er which concludes Plato's *Republic*, though its cosmological and moral basis is rather different; nor does it offer a fully worked-out or comprehensive system of judgement. Only two categories of people are singled out: those whose lives have been dedicated to the pleasures of the flesh are punished after their deaths by extended confinement in the area around the earth before they can return to the heavens (6.29); but

> Nothing which takes place on earth is more agreeable to the leading deity, who rules the entire universe, than gatherings and unions of men joined by law, which are called states; and the guides and preservers of these states, when they depart from them, return here.[59]

Towards the end Africanus reformulates this idea with specific reference to Scipio:

> Exert yourself in the best affairs! And the best cares are those concerning the fatherland: the soul which is driven and exercised by these will fly back to this seat and house more quickly (6.29).[60]

The dichotomy between involvement in public affairs and dedication to pleasure cannot cover all humans; nor does much emerge directly from the Dream about what is involved in being a 'guide and preserver'. But that is not what this section was designed to do: rather, it provides a grand and impressionistic finale to a book whose

77

lost sections, it seems, engaged in detailed and more mundane consideration of how the statesman should behave.

Nonetheless, there are aspects to the telling of the Dream which are suggestive for the reader's understanding of the statesman, particularly in relation to the problem of how the statesman is to sustain his action over an extended period – a problem which the institution of annual magistracies made particularly acute. By separating the rewards for right action from the earthly sphere Cicero is not simply having Scipio utter sentiments which also excuse him, whose popularity and reputation had declined after his consulship; he is also suggesting that the statesman can disregard temporary fluctuations in his standing. The statesman can afford to play the long game – indeed, he is obliged to do so.

The introductory frame to the dream is also worth attention. That Scipio's vision is expounded to him by Africanus reminds the reader of one source of lasting political capital, descent from great men – a factor which is stressed in Africanus' prophecy of Scipio's future, in which he says that Scipio will earn for himself the surname that he has already inherited from Africanus. But one can also ask why Scipio's dream is placed in the context of a visit to the Numidian king Masinissa. Scipio himself is made to explain this as due to the discussion which he and Masinissa had the previous evening about Africanus, but Cicero could have devised other pegs for the episode. What the presence of Masinissa does accomplish is to provide an example of another way that political power at Rome can be sustained over decades. Scipio's grandfather Africanus established close relations with Masinissa during the second Punic war; his grandson has inherited this relationship and maintains it. The meeting with Masinissa is Scipio's initiative, not a chance happening during the campaign. Thus the structure of the dream reminds the reader of Scipio's position within Roman society and thus provides one possible answer to Cicero's ongoing problem of indicating how his statesman is to operate.

On the laws is the most difficult of the three pre-civil war treatises to interpret. Like *On the state*, not all of it survives; unlike *On the state*, it is not clear how many books it contained (since what survives comes only from the first three books) nor indeed whether it was ever completed; as Cicero does not include it in the list of his philosophical works in *On divination*, or refer to it in his letters, it is probable that he did not have copies disseminated and that it only reached the public domain after his death. Thus, whatever Cicero's intentions in composing the work, in practice it is unlikely that it contributed to Cicero's developing persona as a philosophically aware statesman. Nonetheless, it can be argued that *On the laws* marks a further development in Cicero's thinking about the nature and conditions of public life. Its form is significant: for the first time the setting is contemporary, with the speakers being Cicero, his brother Quintus, and Atticus, and there is no frame. The work is not the report of a conversation, but a script of one. By choosing a contemporary setting Cicero is putting himself and his intimates on a par with those involved in the gatherings in 129 and 91 that he described in the earlier works, and by so doing claims a comparable authority and standing. Moreover, the subject of the discussion contributes to the impression that Cicero is now himself exemplifying the continually engaged public figure. The opening conversation quickly leads to a request from Atticus that Cicero write history; Cicero explains that this is not possible at the moment, because he does not have the time. He is relying on the leisure which will accompany old age to give him time to write history, even though he may also be giving legal opinions 'according to the custom of our ancestors' (10). Atticus expresses his doubts that Cicero will ever stop pleading cases, but Quintus expresses enthusiasm, and so their conversation leads to Cicero's agreeing to expound his view of civil law.

The task which the dialogue undertakes is presented at the outset as an activity which is appropriate to a senior figure and in accordance with traditional practice and, according to Quintus, one that, when undertaken by Cicero, will also meet with the approval of the Roman people (12). Cicero has moved, in the course of these dialogues, from considering the problem of the politician to showing what the politician can do: *On the laws* is in some sense the performance of the public figure. And although Cicero places the giving of legal opinions within its Roman tradition, and has Atticus comment on the importance that these studies have had for Cicero since his youth when he studied with the famous jurist Scaevola, he also makes it clear that the normal practice of the jurists is intellectually narrow and too humble for their discussion (14). He will rather offer a philosophical justification for law, and this leads into the discussion proper in book 1. Cicero is drawing attention both to his place within a distinguished Roman tradition and his capacity to transcend what he had inherited through the application of philosophy.

The three pre-civil war treatises are all concerned, then, not only with *how* Rome should be governed but *who* should govern; and although Cicero's discussions are exploratory and not definitive it is clear that one element in a possible answer is continuity. Successful government needs men whose involvement and influence is not limited to their formal periods of office holding; and *On the orator*, at least, considers the contribution that oratory might make to this continued influence.

Running parallel to these thematic links is the shared concern of each work with its own composition and function, articulated through the contrast between *negotium* and *otium*. At the very beginning of *On the orator* Cicero locates his project in the interstices of his public life:

> To me, in my frequent consideration of past time, those men usually seem particularly fortunate, who lived when the state was at its best and, as they flourished in the holding of offices and through the glory of their achievements, were able to pursue a course of life so that they could either enjoy activity (*negotium*) without danger or leisure (*otium*) accompanied by respect; and there was a time when I thought that I too, once the endless work of legal pleading and the pursuit of office had come to a standstill once I had held the public offices and reached a certain age, would be able to embark, with the approval of practically everybody, on a period of rest and of devotion to those fine studies which we both appreciate. But the general troubles of the time, as well as various events which related to me, have frustrated the hope that I had thought and planned for.[61]

Cicero goes on to reflect that throughout his life his enthusiasm for literary study has been interrupted by external events; but that, at the current moment, whatever time he does have he devotes to writing. One could argue that the prime function of this opening is to win the reader's sympathy: composition has been difficult because Cicero has not had adequate leisure. Nonetheless, the terms in which this appeal is case, if that it how it should be read, are not entirely straightforward. Cicero *ought* to have *otium*: that he does not is a reflection upon the unsatisfactory condition of the state. Indeed, the entire work can be seen as a demonstration of how things should be, since it represents senior public figures at leisure and exploring intellectual pursuits: Cicero ought to be in a similar position to Crassus and Antonius. The ultimate effect of the breakdown between *otium* and *negotium* which Cicero here invokes is to bring writing into the public domain: as *otium* is no longer an option for Cicero, those of his activities which in happier circumstances would be the product of *otium* must now be squeezed into the interstices of political activity. Although Cicero makes no explicit claim in the opening of *On the orator* for its public usefulness it is at the least highly suggestive that a work which reflects upon the role of oratory in public life should open with a formulation of its composition which makes its written, as opposed to spoken, words, the product of the busy public man. This is a complex engagement with the boundaries between public and private spheres.

Similar complaints mark the opening of the first book of *On the laws*. The discussion of not writing history revolves around the lack of free and uninterrupted time, *uacuum tempus et liberum*, needed for such an enterprise.[62] When Atticus then asks how Cicero has managed to write anything, he explains that what he has written has been fitted in to the scraps of time that he has had: but 'history can't be begun unless free time has been organised in advance, nor can it be finished quickly'.[63]

These discussions of *otium* take place within the dialogue introductions since they are related to the how and why of each project; and as the opening of *On the state* is lost, it is not clear whether Cicero used a similar line of argument there too. But the earliest stages of that work which survive do introduce the concept of *otium* in terms of a man's duty to serve his country and the superiority of the active over the contemplative life.[64] In particular, we should note the description of the elder Cato – always a loaded point of comparison for his fellow new man – as 'an exemplar of activity and virtue' who 'could have enjoyed himself at leisure at Tusculum'.[65] This is not surprising in itself: the duty of the individual man to engage in constructive activity on behalf of his community could be described as the overall theme of *On the state*. But the active life of *On the state* provides the background against which to set Cicero's own anxieties about leisure and engagement.

The treatises of the late 50s develop the relationship between individual and state, from the specific manifestation of Cicero's own expertise in the form of the orator, through the more general figure of the politically engaged man to the institutional and then specific legal framework in which he operates. And Cicero himself is, in some sense, an example of the kind of man who is needed to make the system work effectively. The anxieties expressed in the introductions about how these works can be written bring in a further dimension to the public figure: but as yet Cicero does not assert that writing itself is an activity which can benefit the state. In the works written during Caesar's dictatorship, however, this move is finally made explicit.

However, before considering further Cicero's development of the idea of writing as an element in the legitimate activity of a public figure, I want to explore another issue which has arisen in this chapter, and that is the articulation in writing of Cicero's relationships with other people. As became clear in the aftermath of the Catilinarian conspiracy, the public figure cannot exist in isolation; and Cicero's works demonstrate his skill at placing himself to advantage.

3

Ciceronian Communities

Roman society was structured around a variety of more or less formal horizontal and vertical relationships. A Roman engaged in public life would be part of a number of networks, some hereditary, some fixed, and others elective and more flexible: relatives by blood and through marriage, clients and patrons whether inherited or incurred, fellow-townsmen and fellow-tribesmen, as well as the whole range of equal and near-equal connections which are designated by *amicitia*.[1] The importance of these bonds in securing political success have long been acknowledged, though the weighting to be given to each in accounting for electoral success is much debated.[2]

In assessing Cicero's place in Roman society one element has been dominant, that of family. This is due in part to the particular importance of family in Roman politics, and more particularly as a result of Cicero's *lack* of blood connections to other Roman politicians. He was a *nouus homo*, a 'new man'; and while there is debate about the precise conditions under which someone could be called a new man, it is absolutely clear that Cicero, none of whose blood relatives had ever been in the Roman senate, could be and was so described. Therefore, to a much greater extent that most of his fellow politicians, Cicero had to create his place within the elite. We have already examined how Cicero used a variety of textual means to manufacture and broadcast his various *personae*. In this chapter, I consider how 'Cicero' is placed in relation to those around him.

It is important to distinguish at the outset between two slightly different ways in which Cicero uses text to place himself in relation to others. On the one hand, there is the making of a permanent record of a event which, in itself, shows Cicero's links with others;

83

on the other, there is the description in a text of a relationship which might not actually exist, or not in the way indicated. When Cicero wrote down and had disseminated a version of a forensic speech which he had already delivered, he was extending and perhaps even modifying the effects of the relationship he had established with his client by means of the original case, but that relationship was already in existence and its fundamental nature had been determined by the act of Cicero as advocate, rather than as a result of the subsequent written version. And this is a different kind of textual relationship from one called into being by letters, by the publication of a speech which was never actually delivered, or by the representation of Cicero's participation in a philosophical dialogue. This group, however much they vary among themselves, share in the characteristic that in each Cicero uses writing to create a community.

Forensic communities

I have already discussed in the Introduction and Chapter 1 the issues surrounding the publication of speeches, forensic and otherwise. Many of the motives for publication concern the image of the speaker: a written version is a permanent record of his competence, whether that competence is to be interpreted as an advertisement for further custom, a demonstration of suitability for office, or even as a pedagogical tool. But a written speech also sets the speaker in a relationship with others, through its record of a set of actions which bind and divide. A forensic case, particularly if successful, establishes for the person defended a permanent obligation towards his or her advocate; and it also leaves a potential for hostility between opposing advocates. When Cicero chose to write down his forensic speeches, he was opting to memorialise a particular relationship.

In Cicero's first case, recorded in *On behalf of Quinctius*, the advocate on the opposing side was Hortensius. Hortensius was still very junior in political terms – he may not even have yet entered the Senate at the time of *On behalf of Quinctius* – but his reputation as an orator was already considerable. Even if the main evidence for his early achievements comes from passages in Cicero's rhetorical works in which Hortensius' career is in counterpoint to Cicero's own, it is nonetheless indisputable that Hortensius, who had made his oratorical debut fourteen years previously, was already one of the outstanding orators at Rome with a number of major successes to his credit.[3] The nearly unknown Cicero uses *On behalf of Quinctius* to establish a relationship with Hortensius and thus enhance his own position. The opening of the speech sets the tone:

> There are two very powerful forces in this country and both are working against us at the moment: great influence and great eloquence. Of the two, Gaius Aquilius, I respect one and fear the other. I am somewhat concerned that the eloquence of Quintus Hortensius may act against me in speaking; and I am truly really rather afraid that the influence of Sextus Naevius may harm Publius Quinctius.[4]

The artfulness of this opening can be unravelled in various ways;[5] for my argument the important point is the position of Hortensius and the suggestion of some form of parity between Hortensius and Cicero. There is a graceful, and no doubt real, respect for Hortensius' abilities, but just as Naevius and Quinctius are matched as plaintiff and defendant, so Hortensius and Cicero are matched as advocates.

As Cicero began to establish his reputation as a forensic speaker his published versions increasingly made their impression through the calibre of the clients: the bald fact of Cicero's speaking could give way to the details of the case. But Cicero remains alert to his relationships with people other than simply his clients.

Politeness to the opposing advocate remains a favoured tactic in certain circumstances: in particular Cicero frequently uses a patronising benevolence towards his opponent where relative ages make that possible and where the prosecutor is a member of the senatorial aristocracy. Torquatus in *On behalf of Sulla*, Laelius in *On behalf of Flaccus*, Laterensis in *On behalf of Plancius* and Atratinus in *On behalf of Caelius* are all treated with courtesy, and their obviously misguided action in prosecuting Cicero's client is explained away in a manner that does not impugn their good faith. In three of the cases there is a solid personal motive behind the prosecution: Torquatus is pursuing a family feud started some years earlier, Laterensis was defeated in the election in which he is claiming Plancius was successful only through bribery, and Atratinus is responding to Caelius' prosecution of his father.[6] And even though Laelius does not have such grounds for prosecuting Flaccus, Cicero makes his respect clear, treating the case as a peculiar aberration.[7] And where his opponents are his equals in age as well as standing politeness is the rule too: the best example of this is the trial of Murena, in which Cicero undermines the case of the prosecution by a genial and devastatingly witty critique of the activities of the prosecutors Servius Sulpicius and the younger Cato. Memmius, the prosecutor of Rabirius Postumus, is misguided: a man who has always been devoted to the Senate's authority should not be involved in this case.[8] But opponents who do not appear as equals do not receive gentle handling. In *On behalf of Flaccus* there is a strong contrast between the noble and misguided Laelius and his two fellow prosecutors Decianus and Herennius Balbus; Decianus in particular is the object of sustained invective.[9] Labienus is stigmatised for cowardice and cruelty in *On behalf of Rabirius accused of high treason*.

Steps can be taken, it would appear, to minimise the ill-feeling that adversarial pleading might engender; though it is not a tactic which Cicero always uses. And indeed it would be wrong to interpret his dealings with opposing advocates solely in terms of his relationships with these men outside, and after, the court case: it is an effective tactic to imply that the prosecution is fissile, as he does in *On behalf of Flaccus*. In *On behalf of Sulla* his mild handling of Torquatus fits with his attempts in that speech, which I discussed in Chapter 2, to counter the accusation that he was abusing his authority in forensic cases. Nonetheless, the written versions of these speeches do show Cicero setting up a group of men, all members of the senatorial aristocracy, to whom he belongs and whose boundaries are delimited through those who, he indicates, do not belong.

The written versions also memorialise Cicero's links with advocates who spoke on the same side as he. It is hardly surprising that he should speak favourably of those with whom he was collaborating but on occasion his remarks are at much greater length than is necessary to indicate how his speech fits into the defence as a whole. *On behalf of Balbus* begins

> If the standing of advocates has any weight at trials, Lucius Cornelius' case is defended by very eminent men; if experience, by very skilled men; if talent, by very eloquent men; if enthusiasm, by very well-disposed men who are linked to Lucius Cornelius both by services rendered and by extremely close friendship.[10]

Cicero goes on then to ask, 'What is my part?', thus implicitly dissociating himself from those whom he has been praising: these turn out to be Marcus Crassus and Gnaeus Pompeius. The first four paragraphs, indeed, are taken up with a laudatory summary of their speeches. Their presence is central to the strategy Cicero adopts in this speech, which is to present Balbus (who is accused of falsely claiming to be a Roman citizen) as the dutiful servant of great Romans whose citizenship is a reward for his services. Indeed, this trial, which took place in 56 shortly after the conference of Luca, is arguably only tangentially about Balbus. It is his position as the friend and confidant of Caesar and the beneficiary of Pompeius' gratitude which makes him the target of the prosecution, and the trial was an attempt to undermine the authority of Pompeius, Caesar and Crassus by an attack on one of their connections – hence the presence at the trial as advocates of those of the three who were then present in Rome. (Caesar was subduing the Veneti.) But we should not assume that Cicero had no choice about the tactics to adopt; he could presumably have constructed a different sort of defence, as indeed he does in *On behalf of Archias*. By giving a speech which foregrounds the presence and speaking of Pompeius and Crassus he is drawing attention to his own relationship with these men – even if, as I have argued elsewhere, he does so in a way which a careful reader could interpret as showing very qualified support for them.[11]

Reinforcing and manipulating networks of power and influence are as much a part of what the written versions of speeches do as is their role in presenting a particular image of Cicero himself. But they can do this because they are based on actual events which themselves had this function. It is now time to consider Cicero's creation of virtual communities in his letters and treatises.

Epistolary communities

The letters are most appropriately treated first, since the community building they seek to effect arises out of pre-existing relationships, however far it may extend them. I raised in the introduction the problems generated by the way in which the letters survived: as they were never 'published' by Cicero, how far can we use them in a study of Cicero's conscious moulding of self? In this chapter, I propose to argue that any solution to this problem must take into account the role of the letters as the concrete representation of complex and on occasion ill-defined communities.

Clearly, we cannot jumble all the letters together and expect useful results from a single approach: the collections are distinct. Most obviously, the hugely diverse set of letters to 'friends' is very different from the collections unified by a single addressee, all of whom were close to Cicero. But we should not necessarily expect that Cicero writes to Atticus in the same way as he does to his brother Quintus, or that either of those correspondences is similar to that with Brutus, separated from Cicero by twenty years of age and a strikingly different political trajectory.

The correspondences with Atticus and with Quintus are arguably of least relevance to this project, given the intimacy and concern for privacy of these letters. There is little sign that Cicero expected what he wrote to become more widely known, even if he occasionally feared that it would. But as one considers the differences in Cicero's relationship with both men, one can see that the letters are fulfilling somewhat different functions. Quintus was arguably the only member of the elite in whom Cicero could have absolute confidence, insofar as their political interests were almost identical; certainly Cicero writes to Quintus in the 50s with apparently uninhibited frankness, even if subsequently the stresses of civil war drove them in different directions.[12] And Cicero could surely not have quite this confidence in Atticus, who was known for his wide range of acquaintances. Despite their connection by marriage, and the undoubted intellectual sympathy between the two, Cicero could not expect the same type of loyalty towards the Tullii Cicerones from Atticus as he could from Quintus. And while Atticus was a valuable confidante precisely because he was not a member of the Senate, and thus in no way a political rival or competitor, Cicero must have been aware that he was a close and valuable friend to others who were senators. Absolute frankness is not to be expected.

An example of the difference in tone between the two correspondences can be found in the descriptions of meetings of the Senate. In writing to Quintus, Cicero gives detailed summaries of when the Senate met and what was discussed, in a compressed and straightforward style. The letters from the 50s, in particular, give the impression that one of their functions was to keep Quintus informed of all public business, even if it was not out of the ordinary or did not concern Cicero directly. Atticus is much less frequently the recipient of such everyday detail, and Cicero's descriptions of senatorial meetings tend to focus around his own performances and concerns.[13] This difference can easily be matched to his correspondents' interests. Quintus was himself a senior figure, even at one point a plausible candidate for the consulship, whose absences from Rome were on official business. Atticus was not a member of the Senate, and moreover was someone who had made it clear that he was not interested in participation in public life.

It is possible to go beyond the observation that Cicero is more reserved to Atticus than to his brother and consider that the one function of the letters to Atticus is the constant reassertion of the close relationship between them. Nor should we assume that Cicero was, or felt himself to be, always the senior partner. In addition to his consciousness that Atticus was linked closely with many other people was the nature of their own relationship, which had begun when they were adolescents: at that period Atticus' being three years older would have been a significant difference. And during Atticus' long absence in Greece they had little opportunity to become close. The first surviving letter, from 68, is indeed rather stiff and awkward, not least because the marriage between Quintus Cicero and Pomponia was clearly already in trouble and Cicero was feeling the need to defend his brother.[14] He also justifies in some detail the steps he has been taking in relation to a business commission from Atticus. The letter is perfectly friendly, but there is nothing in it to suggest exceptional friendship; nor indeed would one be certain from it alone that the marriage connection had not generated the friendship, whereas it seems in fact that Cicero and Atticus promoted the match because they were already close.

Friendships change over time, and the relative distance of the early letters need not be a model for this friendship's workings subsequently. But, even if the correspondence with Atticus is private and intimate, that does not necessarily mean that Cicero is not concerned about the impression he makes upon Atticus, and of the need to present himself in such a way in his letters as to maintain his place in Atticus' range of connections, not all of whom were necessarily friends of Cicero.[15]

These reflections on Cicero's correspondence with Atticus cannot be more than speculation, particularly in the absence of any replies. It is much clearer that some, at least, of the letters to friends are written in the consciousness of Cicero's place within a wider community.

A good starting point is Cicero's correspondence with Caelius in 51-50 BC.[16] Caelius starts his first letter by referring to a promise to tell Cicero was is going on:

When we parted I promised that I would write to you with great care about all the affairs of the city, and I have taken steps to find someone who will follow everything up – to the extent that I'm afraid that the care will seem far too painstaking. Nonetheless I know how inquisitive you are and how pleasurable it is for all travellers to be told about even the most trivial things which are happening at home.[17]

This is a correspondence about news – even if Caelius has delegated the actual information gathering to unnamed *operarii*, 'hirelings'. But Cicero's response suggests otherwise:

What! Do you think I asked you to send me the pairings in gladiatorial combats, postponed court appearances, Chrestus' burglary and everything else which no one would dare tell me in Rome?[18]

And he goes on to explain that what he wants from Caelius is analysis of the likely course of future events. It is not that he is not interested in Caelius' resumes of events, but rather that the supply of information is not a problem. 'Others will write, many will bring news, even rumour itself will deliver much information.'[19] This remark is highly significant, since it demonstrates that Cicero's information service, even at a considerable distance from Rome, was so good that he did not need to rely any specific informant. But at the same time incisive *analysis* of public events from one involved in them was extremely valuable.[20]

Caelius' readiness to expend time and money in supplying Cicero with accurate news can be understood within a context of patronage and the exchange of services. In 51, the balance of services rendered was very much on Cicero's side: in addition to the normal expectation of gratitude towards a senior figure who was providing support and encouragement towards a young man entering public life, Cicero had literally been Caelius' *patronus* at his trial, on the capital charge of *uis*, five years earlier.[21] Caelius had so far limited opportunities to respond, and it is possible to see his epistolary response to this particular request from Cicero as deliberately excessive, an extravagant gesture to demonstrate his commitment to the relationship: particularly as he hoped for more favours in the immediate future.[22] And from Cicero's point of view, the incommensurability of the relationship was precisely what made Caelius so valuable an informant: Cicero could not expect frank exchanges with his peers, and turned for news to men whose age meant they were not in direct competition with him.

This correspondence can be viewed, then, as an extension of the relationship of patronage and friendship which existed between Caelius and Cicero: a playing out in the epistolary sphere of sentiments and obligations which would still have been operating had both been in Rome, though the actions engendered would have been different. But if this correspondence was in any way not private its place in Cicero's relationship networks has further resonances; so it is worth considering the ways in which a correspondence can be open to persons other than sender and recipient.

Crucially, openness to others is a sliding scale rather than an absolute. At one end is a correspondence whose very existence is known, at the time, only to the two correspondents; at the other, letters which are no sooner received by, or even sent to, their recipient than they are made available without restriction to a wider community. In between, there are many possible permutations: letting the fact of correspondence be known, but keeping all contents a secret; offering summaries of contents, without disseminating verbatim passages; revealing selected passages from letters sent or received, but keeping other parts secret; passing around the original, or copies, to selected individuals. And all these possibilities are compounded by the knowledge or otherwise of the other party to the original correspondence: we shall read differently a letter written in the expectation that it will remain private, where this expectation is frustrated, from one written in the expectation that it will be read by others in addition to its nominal recipient.

Cicero and his correspondents did not have available the positions at both ends of the scale. It would not be possible, in the absence of a depersonalised postal service, to be completely sure that the fact of the transmission of a letter had remained secret, even if seals could keep the contents safe; and public dissemination was limited by the scope of copying and distribution technologies, quite apart from issues of literacy. As I discussed in Chapter 1, epistolary privacy is not a straightforward issue.

In the case of correspondence with Caelius, it is difficult to see why Caelius should keep the *fact* of his correspondence with Cicero a secret: why should he not advertise his closeness to Cicero? And we can at least speculate that Caelius discussed the contents of Cicero's letters with close friends. It would seem unlikely, at any rate, that Cicero could rely on Caelius' silence – and at points he does seem to choose discretion over complete frankness.[23] But it would be wrong to assume that a degree of openness was necessarily a disadvantage. Through his correspondence with Caelius, Cicero is not only keeping in touch with events in Rome: he is demonstrating that he is keeping in touch with events in Rome, and for a man who was peculiarly sensitive to the dangers of being absent from Rome, that was as important a goal as being well-informed.[24]

The letters to Caelius show the mechanics of patronage working in epistolary form. Elsewhere, we can see letters matching up to particular events in which relationships were called upon, and providing substitutes for the concrete meetings. One type of letter in which this is very clear is the letter of recommendation.[25] All the letters of recommendation in the *Letters to Friends* collection are to men geographically separate from Cicero: they are substitutes for face-to-face meetings.[26] They are also entirely pointless without other people, above all the third party named in the letter. Consider a letter to Acilius, a governor of Sicily:

> Gaius Flavius, a respected and distinguished Roman knight, is a great friend of mine: he was very close to my son-in-law Gaius Piso and both he and his brother Lucius Flavius pay their respects scrupulously to me. So please, for my sake, deal with Gaius Flavius as finely and generously as you are able, in so far as that accords with you honour and dignity. Nothing could possibly be more welcome to me. Moreover, I promise you (I say this not from interested motives, but as the result of our friendship and connection and also since it is the truth) that Gaius Flavius' dutifulness, attentiveness, and above all the high standing and influence he has among his own circle will be a source of great pleasure to you. Goodbye.[27]

This type of letter is about creating and strengthening social relations, in the first instance between the third party and the recipient but also between Cicero and the two others. He frequently acknowledges that showing favour to the person he names is also a favour to *him*;[28] and he also on occasion asks the recipient to indicate, should the desired *rapprochement* with the third-party come about (or that the favour requested has been granted), that Cicero's letter has played a part.[29] This is a triangular form of communication; and although there is an actual outcome which the person recommended wants, and in which he may be disappointed, Cicero has fulfilled his obligation by writing the letter. The favour done by Cicero is not negated if the recommendation does not work.

The letter to Acilius about the Flavii brothers is a straightforward example. Things can be more complicated. In 56 BC Cicero wrote to the governor of Africa, Q. Valerius Orca, asking that he be well disposed towards the connections in Africa of a man called Publius Cuspius, and then specifies one in particular, a L. Iulius, for Orca's benevolence.[30] The web of obligations here has four points rather than three. Orca, should he accede to Cicero's request, will oblige three individuals; Iulius will be obligated to three; and Cicero and Cuspius will both have received and done a favour. And while a web is one analogy for these communications, another is a ladder, inasmuch as Iulius approaches his target, the governor of the province in which he has business, through two intermediaries rather than just one.

The first paragraph indicates that this letter continues an earlier conversation between Cicero and Orca about Cuspius, when Orca was about to depart for his province, and that the subject has already been mentioned in Cicero's letters. Then, having rehearsed the arguments on behalf of Cuspius, Cicero says that in future letters he will simply put a mark against the name of any who is connected with Cuspius. There is no parallel for this mechanism elsewhere in the correspondence (though Cicero does occasionally show a weakness for elementary cryptography);[31] it would appear to be an attempt to streamline the process of recommendation, by establishing a shorthand for endlessly repetitive and highly formalised recommendations for Cuspius' associates. It is impossible to know whether Cicero adopted it; *Fam.* 13.6a would suggest not, but equally the subsequent editor might not have felt such abbreviated letters worth including.

The formalisation of this type of letter is a concern also when Cicero turns to the specific recommendation of Iulius. He says that Cuspius has asked him to recommend Iulius with such enthusiasm that normal expressions are inadequate, and that he has promised Cuspius that he will use his skills to produce 'an amazing kind of recommendation'.[32] He then explains to Orca that he cannot do such a thing, but asks that Orca's response give the impression of being caused by an extraordinary letter. This is rhetorically effective, not only in demonstrating the intensity of Cicero's support for Cuspius but also in its attempt to create a bond, through a shared, benevolent deception, between Cicero and Orca. Nonetheless, Cicero does not commit himself to much concerning Iulius. His claims to Orca's attention rely solely on his connection with Cuspius: he is 'eminently worthy' of Orca's friendship because Cuspius has told Cicero that this is the case, and Cicero knows of Cuspius' judgement in choosing his friends.[33] There is plenty of opportunity for Orca to come to his own conclusions about Iulius. But Cicero does press the obligation firmly on Orca, reminding him in the opening paragraph that they have already discussed the matter and saying, at the end, 'I shall judge the effect of this letter in the immediate future and I have every expectation of thanking you.'[34] He then says that he will take care of Orca's affairs in Rome. On one level this is merely the offer of reciprocal favours, but the scrutiny of Orca's actions is closer than is usual in letters of recommendation. One reading might be that Cicero *is* genuinely and strongly concerned for the interests of Cuspius and his friends. But it is also possible that Cicero had doubts about the security of this letter, and wished to give the appearance of sincere support should its contents become more widely disseminated. We do not know, after all, what he may have said to Orca on the subject at their face-to-face meeting.

It is impossible to determine which line of interpretation is more plausible in the absence of any other knowledge of these individuals and their circumstances. Cuspius and Iulius are not mentioned elsewhere in the letters; there are a couple of further letters to Orca from the Caesarian period, both from book 13 and concerning the land redistributions, which are inevitably a less than sure indication of their relationship, and Orca appears elsewhere in Cicero's writings only as one of the praetors of 57, mentioned towards the end of the duty thanks in his speech of thanks on his return to the Senate.

Letters to Friends 13.6 is self-conscious both of its genre and of its audiences, but it is still nonetheless a letter of recommendation. The same is hardly true of one to Caesar from 45 BC, in which the ostensible commendation – Cicero urges Caesar to show favour to one Precilius – seems simply to be a vehicle for the oblique transmission of a rather different message.[35] It is a very peculiar letter of recommendation: indeed Cicero concludes, 'I have used a new kind of letter to you so that you might understand my recommendation is not of the ordinary kind.'[36] The person he is recommending is already closely connected with Caesar – his father is described as a *necessarius* of Caesar – and he tried to get Cicero to join Caesar's side. And for much of the letter Cicero justifies his own conduct in taking the side of Caesar's opponents while claiming that he has no ambition now. He demonstrates this change in his own attitudes through a series of Greek quotations, moving from 'Homeric magniloquence' to describe his futile search for glory during the civil war to Euripides to describe his current prudence. No other letter of recommendation includes literary quotations, either in Latin or Greek; nor does the other letter of recommendation from Cicero to Caesar in this book show any notable signs of divergence from the conventions of the genre.

Shackleton Bailey offers a convincing explanation for Cicero's motives in the context of early summer 45: this letter is a response to rumours which had reached Caesar that Cicero was not trustworthy, and Cicero chose to write in this way in order to counter the rumours without explicitly having to admit their existence. But Shackleton Bailey's surprise that Cicero chose to do so via a *commendatio* is perhaps misplaced. The letter of recommendation had two particular advantages. It allowed two individuals to negotiate their relationship through the oblique medium of their attitudes towards a third;[37] and, at least in Cicero's hands, its generic conventions were already capable of being invoked as a model against which particular digressions could become significant.

Whereas the distance between correspondents is, in letters of recommendation, merely the cause of the information being conveyed by letter (rather, say, than orally) in the series of letters to exiles which Cicero wrote following the civil war separation is at the heart of the correspondence. There are some twenty-five letters of advice and consolation to men who had fought with Pompeius and were still as a result absent from Rome;[38] the shared characteristics of these letters was clearly apparent to the initial editor, since the majority are gathered into book 6 of the collection.

3. Ciceronian Communities

While the letters of recommendation operate within a network of social relations based on patronage, these letters of consolation presuppose an equality of standing between writer and recipient. And the importance of the letter form is different too. The letters of recommendation can be seen as substitutes for a face-to-face meeting in which the same information might have been conveyed; epistolary conventions affect the form of the message, but the letter itself is used simply because, in these particular cases, Cicero could not give the message orally. There are no surviving letters of recommendation written when both Cicero and his correspondent are in Rome. But in the case of the letters of consolation to exiles the letter form is fundamental to what Cicero has to say, since the basis of the correspondence is, ultimately, that the recipients are *not* in Rome – and that Cicero himself is. It is from his perspective as a man returned to the heart of Caesar's empire that he offers advice, and his standing as adviser is confirmed from the outset by his success in adapting to the new political situation.

These letters, despite their diverse addressees, contain very similar material.[39] Two strands dominate: advice and sympathy. The dichotomy appears most clearly in a letter to Toranius which begins 'Two days ago I gave Gnaeus Plancius' slaves a letter to you, so I shall now be more succinct and, whereas earlier I wrote to console you, now I shall offer advice.'[40] Cicero offers consolation derived from various sources. For some correspondents, it has clear philosophical origins: death is not to be feared,[41] the wise man must yield to circumstances,[42] there is nothing which can cause fear except for the consciousness of wrongdoing.[43] In other cases, it is practical: a desire to be in Rome is misplaced;[44] or recall is imminent. It can be observed, then, that the focus of consolation wavers between the specific (with these correspondents, the fact of continuing exile) and general lamentations about the civil war and its consequences. Sometimes, Cicero disclaims consolation, either because it is not needed or because he has none to offer.[45] Inability to offer consolation can be connected with the more general trope of being unable to write at all;[46] which itself on occasion shades into an inability to write that is specific to Cicero. Recurrent in his consolations on the general situation is the idea that any prospect of an ultimately satisfying outcome to the current political instability is impossible, and above all, victory by the anti-Caesarian forces (a real concern at some moment, particularly in the spring of 45) will not necessarily lead to improvement. That is, the situation is either unrelievedly gloomy,[47] or Caesarian victory has ceased to be inevitably the worse outcome.

His advice is normally to suggest passivity. His correspondents must accept the situation as it is, though they are encouraged to hope for a restoration from Caesar. And just as on occasion he claims to be unable to offer consolation, so sometimes he says that advice is beyond him.[48] The giving of advice often brings the focus of the letter back onto Cicero. In part this is because he often promises to act as mediator between his correspondent and Caesar in order to secure a return for the exile.[49] But sometimes Cicero indicates that he had been able to foresee the course of events leading up to and through the civil war, and his resulting ability to modify his behaviour, even if it led to obloquy at the time, contributes to his capacity to give advice now.[50] Foresight claimed with hindsight can be difficult to distinguish from self-justification, and there are times in these letters where Cicero's main aim seems to be to convince his correspondent that the course of action which he, Cicero, took during the civil war, is acceptable.[51]

These letters, then, are highly repetitive; they are also as much about Cicero as they are about his correspondents' situations. They are not concerned with conveying particular information. Once Cicero claims to have delayed writing in the hope that good news might be imminent;[52] though in fact none has come, and he does not explain why he has nonetheless chosen to write. Rather, he is conveying, and repeating, his support for these individuals throughout their period of exile. The letters are tangible signs of his continuing goodwill; they are also demonstrations of his recovered status in Rome (despite his disclaimers) insofar as he can claim to have some influence over the course of events.[53]

To that extent, this set of letters might be regarded merely as illustrating, over an extended compass, Cicero's interest in community building and in inserting himself within networks, demonstrated through a kind of letter (consolation to an exile) which is represented elsewhere in the *Letters to Friends* collection. But Cicero's presentation of self and use of letters takes on a further dimension in the context of the aftermath of the civil war. He is advocating a profound political quietism, and attempting to dissuade his correspondents from maintaining any hope in the results of a Pompeian victory; moreover, he proves himself to be something of an apologist for Caesar, or at least for Caesar's merciful side – which is itself set off by the contrast with the shadowy horrors which, it is suggested, might follow or have followed a Pompeian victory.[54] In effect, then, Cicero is – whether consciously or not – taking a significant political stand in his demonstration of how a senior figure, one formerly Pompeian, can co-exist with Caesar. This co-existence is not rendered null by the frequent lamentations for what has been lost: there is no pretence that the *res publica* remains, and Cicero's attitude toward the future wavers during the period, but a constant through the letters is that, however painful, it is nonetheless possible to live in Rome under Caesar and indeed that this is a situation to which his exiled friends can reasonably aspire.

This emerges most strikingly from the letters from Cicero to M. Marcellus, who had remained in exile in Mytilene after Pharsalus. The problem here was not that he wished to return to Rome, and that his wish was frustrated, but that he appeared not to want to return at all. *Fam.* 4.7-9 are attempts to persuade Marcellus that he should be prepared to come back to Rome.[55] In order to effect this, Cicero needs to get Marcellus to make a radical change in his behaviour without impugning his past conduct. This can involve tortuous locutions: consider, for example, the opening sentence of 4.7:

> Even though I gather that you still hold to an opinion which I would not dare to criticise (not because I do not disagree with it, but because I have such a regard for your wisdom that I would not place my judgement before yours) nonetheless our long-standing friendship and your great goodwill towards me (which I have been aware of since your childhood) have encouraged me to write to you about those matters which I think concern your safety and which I consider do not conflict with your standing.[56]

Cicero's difficulties are compounded by his own behaviour: he, unlike Marcellus, has chosen to accept Caesar's pardon, to return to Rome and even, by the time of these letters, to take part in public life once more. Cicero's authority, in general and as an adviser to Marcellus, depends at least in part on the correctness of this decision; indeed, he offers himself as a model to Marcellus of how to serve the changed *res publica*.[57] He needs, therefore, to find a formula which will justify the course of action of both of them. He does so via a restatement both of the past and of the present.

As far as the civil war goes, he suggests that Marcellus distrusted from the outset Pompeius' strategy and forces and had as little to do with the fighting as possible; and that in this he was at one with Cicero.[58] The gap between them arose only when hope of victory for Pompeius' side had gone. Marcellus has taken a third path, unlike both those who have continued the fight and those (including Cicero) who have 'trusted themselves to the victor'.[59] Cicero seeks to close that gap, in effect, with the argument that there is now no significant difference between his position and Marcellus', since he cannot escape Caesar simply by being absent from Rome: 'you should consider that, wherever you are, you will be in the power of him whom you flee.'[60] As this is the case, there is no particular reason to avoid Rome; and it is the background to the positive suggestion, that, provided there is some form of commonwealth, Marcellus ought to be a *princeps* therein.[61] Cicero supports the argument that Marcellus should return by expressing concerns about the damage that his absence is causing his property.

A number of features are noteworthy here. It hardly needs to be said that Cicero avoids entirely a direct engagement with Marcellus' reasons for absence, namely a refusal to come to any accommodation with Caesar's regime. We might think that Cicero does not want to acknowledge the strength of this position by actually stating it, even though a number of his points obliquely address it (Rome is as good a place as any other to be an exile, Caesar's power extends throughout the world). It is also worth looking beyond the mechanics of persuasion to the fact itself of persuasion. The other letters to Pompeian exiles are about reconciling their correspondents with the status quo and to accept that any change in it will be brought about by the efforts of other people: they advocate passivity. Marcellus, however, needs to be stirred to action, or at least to a public acknowledgement that he will accept mercy, should it be offered.[62] Why is Cicero so concerned to get Marcellus back to Rome? The answer must lie in Marcellus' status, and the reflection which his behaviour cast upon Cicero's. There were few pre-civil war consulars left alive who had been on the Pompeian side; just as Marcellus' remaining in Mytilene suggested that Cicero had been pusillanimous to make his peace with Caesar, so Marcellus' return would confirm the rightness of Cicero's taking a part, once again, in public life. The case of Marcellus provided, in fact, one of Cicero's few public outings during Caesar's dictatorship: the *pro Marcello* is the only speech he delivered in the Senate during this period.[63] We can connect this attitude to Marcellus with a greater optimism on Cicero's part in late 46 about the position of the *res publica*; if he foresaw for himself some form of public prominence, then it becomes clearer why it is so important to justify his past actions and to acquire such allies as he can.

Important confirmation of Cicero's consciousness of the need for self-justification comes in a letter to Marcus Marius (*Fam.* 7.3). Marius was an old friend of Cicero's, not involved in politics: two letters to him survive from the pre-civil war period, one a charmingly mannered description of the games held when Pompeius' theatre complex was opened in 55, and the other a gossipy note about Cicero's forensic activities from early in 51 before he left from Cilicia.[64] The third in the sequence, datable to some time in 46, lacks the earlier light-heartedness. Cicero starts by recollecting the last time he and Marius met: on 12 May 49 BC. He recalls Marius' anxieties about his, Cicero's, position: 'if I stayed in Italy, you were afraid that I should be shirking my duty; but if I set out for war, the danger I would be in alarmed you.'[65] Cicero acknowledges that he did not know what to do then, but explains that he chose to value his honour and reputation rather than his safety. He proceeds to explain why he came to regret his choice to accompany Pompeius, because of the kind of people he found on the same side and because his advocacy of peace failed to produce any effect. When Pompeius lost the war, Cicero abandoned the conflict. He lists six possible alternatives open 'if you did not want, or did not dare, to entrust yourself to the victor':[66] exile was the most attractive of these. He then changes tack: the next sentence, in asyndeton, begins 'I came home, …'. There was no reason for him to commit suicide, though plenty of reasons why he should desire to; there is consolation in innocence, in his intellectual pursuits, and in the glory of his past achievements. He then apologises for writing at length and recapitulates his position: opposition to individuals becoming greater that the state; when this had happened, the advocacy of peace; and finally, being a citizen, if Rome is a *ciuitas* and if not, being an exile.

Up to this point the letter handles familiar themes: the anxieties about Pompeius' tactics and associates are in the letters to Atticus in 49, and the self-justification here is very similar to that in the letters to Pompeian exiles. It is undoubtedly a powerfully affecting piece of writing: not simply in the unity of language and emotion but also in the apparently inescapable explanatory aporia into which Cicero has fallen as he attempts to explain why he has returned to Rome, despite the seemingly endless list of alternatives to that course of action which he presents. And were this letter to conclude at the end of section 5, there would be some grounds – its rhetorical skill, its detailed self-justification, and even its precise recollection of the time and place of their last meeting – for thinking that Cicero might have expected, or even desired, Marius to convey its contents further. And in fact, that is precisely what Cicero says explicitly in the next paragraph. 'I would have preferred to discuss these things with you directly; but since time was passing, I wanted to do so in a letter, so that you would have something to say if you ever came across my detractors. For there are people who think it grounds for accusation that I am alive – even though my death would have been of no use to the commonwealth; and I am certain the death-roll does not seem long enough to them.'[67] His letter is to provide Marius with his script when he meets someone who criticises Cicero's course of conduct.

In these letters Cicero is taking one group, that of Pompeian exiles, and attempting to modify it into a community of men who wish to find a place for themselves in the new Caesarian dispensation and whose desire to do so responds to Cicero's advice and support.

3. Ciceronian Communities

Communication, not action, is the heart of Cicero's exhortations: the transformation in the exiles' position depends on Caesar. It is the image of activity which these letters project which is crucial. The final epistolary community I shall consider is different: it is the group of men to whom Cicero wrote in 44-43, as he attempted to orchestrate the opposition to Marcus Antonius.

Three of the sixteen volumes of *Letters to Friends* (10-12) fall into this category, as do the surviving letters to Marcus Brutus: about one hundred and twenty letters in all, that is over a quarter of all of Cicero's surviving letters to correspondents other than Atticus and his brother Quintus. Moreover, quite a number of these letters are to Cicero, or indeed to the Senate and people of Rome, rather than from him: the impression given by the original editor's choices of what to include is that Cicero is at the centre of a web of communications.

This impression is one reinforced by Cicero's own use of the epistolary form. It is not simply that the letters, transcending any purely personal connection between the two ostensible parties, are designed to reinforce the community which Cicero is attempting to maintain in 44 and 43, of men who manifest their support for a free state by means of unremitting hostility to Marcus Antonius; in addition, they refer back to this community in order to make the message work. It is by communicating news of this group of like-minded in action that the group will continue to function.

These letters comprise a number of distinct correspondences with magistrates located across the Empire. There are letters to and from Plancus, the governor of Transalpine Gaul (*Fam.* 10.1-24) with a pair from Cicero to one of his legates, Furnius (10.25-6); to and from Lepidus, the governor of Narbonese Gaul and nearer Spain (10.27, 10.34-5) and to and from Pollio, the governor of further Spain (10.31-3); between Cicero and Decimus Brutus, governor of Cisalpine Gaul (11.4-26), him and Cassius, governor of Syria (12.1-13) and with Cornificius, governor of Africa (12.17-30) as well as the separate correspondence with Marcus Brutus, the governor of Macedonia. There is a letter from Trebonius, then governor of Asia, (12.16) and one from Cicero to him (10.28), though Trebonius had been assassinated long before the letter could have reached him; an account from Galba, a legate of the consul Pansa, of the battle of Mutina (10.30); a dispatch from Lentulus Spinther, proquaestor with propraetorian rank in Asia, to the Senate, with a covering letter for Cicero (12.14-15); and a letter from Decimus Brutus to Cassius and Marcus Brutus, and a pair from the latter to Marcus Antonius (11.1-3). There is also a note of reassurance from Cicero to Appius Claudius (10.29) after the latter had been declared a public enemy, included no doubt because Cicero refers to the matter in a letter to Decimus Brutus. The final items in these three books, a letter from Cicero to Oppius, from July 44 (11.29); and an exchange of letters with Matius (11.30-31), are from the same period but anomalous for my purposes, since neither correspondent was a magistrate; the connection is rather that these letters too deal explicitly with the aftermath of Caesar's assassination. Setting them aside, however, we have here Cicero in correspondence, often reciprocal, with all the significant military figures at the time, with the exception of Octavian (Cicero's letters to whom were gathered in a separate collection, now lost) and Marcus Antonius.

It is not ultimately a factual correspondence. Cicero is not really concerned to give a detailed account of what has been going on in Rome, nor does he give much in the way of specific advice on particular issues. In large part this is due to the nature of communication by letter, for there were enormous time-lags in delivery. There would be no point in Cicero trying to tell commanders on the ground what to do, since he had little idea, when he wrote, where they were or what conditions they faced. But Cicero's apparent reluctance to give details about Rome is more striking, particularly as he often draws attention to the gap. His assumption is always that his correspondent has other sources of information.[68] This is interesting confirmation of what Cicero himself said while governor of Cilicia, but it perhaps has further significance: by drawing attention to other sources of information Cicero is showing that both his correspondent and he are part of a wider network of information exchange.

Rather, Cicero's main purpose in the letters is hortatory: his correspondents must continue their struggle against Marcus Antonius, and are encouraged to do so by an appeal to the reputation which they will acquire should they so act. 'You need no encouragement, any more than you needed it in that action of yours, the greatest in human memory [sc. the assassination of Caesar]; but let me nonetheless remind you that the Roman people are looking to you for everything and place every hope of some day regaining their freedom in you.'[69] 'By the immortal gods, throw yourself into those careful considerations which will bring you the greatest standing and glory; and there is only one path to glory – above all at this point, when the state has been harassed for so many years – good states-manship.'[70] Cicero articulates his appeals through established norms of public approbation; he takes the ostensibly private medium of the letter and makes it act as the public arena at Rome.

Moreover, this correspondence is full of other writings and opin-ions; I touched on the *Philippics'* concern with other texts in Chapter 1. Cicero writes to Cassius that he is 'delighted that my speech and motion met with your approval' and goes on to discuss its origins and effects in more detail (he is referring to the first *Philippic*).[71] He hopes that other people will tell Decimus Brutus about his delivery of the third and fourth *Philippics*[72] and Cornificius about the third,[73] and promises to send Marcus Brutus the eleventh.[74] He tells Plancus how a letter of his has been received in the Senate,[75] and likewise to Cornificius[76] and Brutus;[77] and explains to Plancus that he has shared the contents of a letter from him with a large number of people, to general delight;[78] he discusses this same letter with Mar-cus Brutus, who has received a copy, and compares it Plancus' behaviour with that of Lepidus, with which he expects Brutus to be familiar from letters from his connections.[79] Marcus Brutus conveys his delight in the fifth and seventh *Philippics*.[80] And the circle is completed in the *Philippics*: the tenth and thirteenth of the series are contributions to debates held in the Senate in response to letters received from Brutus and from Lepidus. And breakdowns in episto-lary communication are matters for concern: so Asinius Pollio complains of the length of time that it takes for letters to reach him in Spain,[81] and Cicero explains to Marcus Brutus that they have received no letters from Cassius.[82]

The textual overload of 44-43 is on one level a direct response to the highly complex geopolitical situation; or, in other words, the mechanisms of city-state government could not cope with a Mediterranean empire. The slippage between the formal locus of decision-making at Rome and the actual events in such widely separated areas is mediated by the exchange of texts; yet the inevitable time-lag results in the constant sense, in this part of Cicero's correspondence, of letters passing in transit, of information reaching its recipients too late, of a profound failure of communication. And yet the significance of these letters is not just as an index of the Roman world's inadequate infrastructure. As I have discussed, Cicero frequently disclaims a factual motive. These letters are rather about insisting to his correspondents on the need for a particular course of action, and what backs up that insistence is both Cicero's own authority, which he explains that he is also manifesting in the Senate through his speeches, and his location of himself and each of his correspondents within a wider network of right thinking Roman citizens, who are watching what is going on and making their opinions known. Letters, then, become the means whereby the regulating gaze of the Roman citizen body, with its implications for advancement and standing, is extended beyond the city to the Empire in its entirety.

Such, at least, was Cicero's intention. But he could not keep all his correspondents in line: as the situation became clearer in the aftermath of the battles of Mutina, key figures – Lepidus above all, but also Plancus and eventually Pollio – opted to support Marcus Antonius. Cicero failed; his textual presence was ultimately not compelling enough. But more interesting are both the extent to which, in the period before military action had overtaken words, he did manage to preserve the possibility of success; and the extent to which failure is already a matter he is contemplating in the *Philippics*, and earlier – an idea to which I return in the final chapter.

Intellectual communities

In his speeches and letters Cicero is using forms of social interaction which were embedded in Roman elite society. His treatises, too, can be seen in this context through their explicit relationship with a particular reader. In *On the orator* and *On the state* Cicero, when speaking in his own voice, is addressing his remarks to his brother Quintus; in the later treatises, Marcus Brutus performs that role in

Brutus, On ends, Tusculan disputations, and *On the nature of the gods,* Atticus does so in *Laelius on friendship* and *Cato on old age* and Cicero's son Marcus in *On duties.* This is clearly a form of dedication, but it is a relaxed and informal one: even in *On duties,* where Cicero starts by explaining to his son how this work may fit into his studies in Athens, the impression is conversational. It is as though other readers are being permitted to overhear a discussion between friends: philosophy is being presented as the leisure activity of the elite, thus substantiating the claims about *otium* which the prefaces often articulate. Nor does there seem to be a sharp distinction between these treatises and the ones which do not have a named reader. *On the laws* does not, because it is entirely in dialogue form with no frame in Cicero's own voice; and *On divination* is presented as a conversation which developed between Cicero and Quintus.

The one case which is slightly different is the *Academica.* This, the second in the series of philosophical treatises after the civil war, posed considerable problems for Cicero in terms of its presentation, and eventually generated two editions. Cicero's initial plan was to use the same interlocutors as in *Hortensius*; however, as he wrote the new and more demanding work, he came to the conclusion that Hortensius, Catulus and Lucullus could not plausibly be in command of its philosophical content. He therefore devised a second version, in which the speakers were himself, Atticus, and Marcus Terentius Varro.[83] He also wrote a dedicatory letter to Varro to accompany the second edition.[84]

It seems likely that this covering letter was intended for dissemination: Cicero certainly sent a copy to Atticus at the same time as to Varro, asking for his reaction to it and exclaiming at the amount of effort its composition had cost him. In it Cicero places his four books into a potentially reciprocal relationship with those that Varro is writing (*On the Latin language*) which he had promised to dedicate to Cicero. Cicero explains that he had hoped to delay the dissemination of his own work until after Varro's had appeared, but as this has not happened – and he ascribes Varro's slowness to the care that he is taking – he will let his work emerge nonetheless, in order 'to advertise our shared intellectual interests and mutual affection'.[85]

Dedications emphasise the existence of a mutually supportive network of men engaged in intellectual pursuits.

At the same time, however, the letter indicates the limits of this intellectual community, since Cicero warns Varro about the role which he plays in the philosophical discussion: 'I expect that you'll be surprised, when you read it, at our talking about matters which we never talked about – but you know how dialogues work.'[86] The *Academica* is thus explicitly fictional, at least as far as its content goes; what the letter implies, however, is that mutual goodwill and intellectual prowess which the dialogue manifests are not fictional, since Cicero then looks forward to conversations which he and Varro may have in the future. And the letter concludes with reflections on the unsatisfactory political situation and the value and attractiveness of literary studies in such a climate; we have here the nexus, familiar from the prefaces to the treatises, of political unemployment and the writing of texts.

The ideal of an intellectual community was clearly attractive to Cicero but its implementation was apparently problematic. At least, the formal dedicatory letter of the *Academica* is not repeated elsewhere; nor does Cicero again include Varro as a speaker in his dialogues, restricting himself thereafter to his brother Quintus, Atticus and (in *On fate*) Hirtius as living interlocutors. Cicero's effort in creating intellectual communities in his treatises is in fact directed more towards the groups of men which he sites in the past. One element, indeed, in the distinctive flavour of the Ciceronian philosophical dialogue is the recreation of specific time, place, and group of people:[87] and I suggest that the motives determining this choice include Cicero's desire to extend the community to which he belongs back in time. These *mises-en-scène* are not simply an alternative history of Rome of general application, though that is certainly an element in their force; they are also Cicero's personal history, and the individuals involved are metaphorical forebears whom Cicero can claim as a result of his own actions. Thus the writing of the treatises is a way in which Cicero can compensate for his lack of prestigious biological forebears.

Not all of Cicero's treatises are in dialogue form nor are all his dialogues set in the past. The relevant ones are *On the orator* (91 BC);

3. Ciceronian Communities

On the state (129 BC); *Hortensius* (between 65 and 61 BC); the
first edition of the *Academica* (between 62 and 60 BC); *On ends*
(books 1-2, 50 BC; books 3-4, 52 BC; book 5, 79 BC); *On the
nature of the gods* (76 BC); *Cato on old age* (150 BC) and *Laelius*
(129 BC).[88] There is clearly wide variation among this category,
and further divisions are helpful: in particular, one can distinguish
between treatises in which Cicero represents himself as recollecting
a conversation in which he himself participated at some point in the
past (which may be as close to the present as the first two books of
On ends, recalling events only five years earlier, or as distant as the
final book of that work, over thirty years previous to the date of
composition), and those where Cicero was not present, and his
account is based on what others have told him. Four fall into this
latter category: *On the orator*, *On the state*, *Cato on old age* and
Laelius.

It is striking that Cicero chose in his initial attempts at treatise
writing, *On the orator* and *On the state*, to describe the remoter past.
Moreover, in these two works he also employs a distinctly larger
number of characters than in the later treatises: seven in *On the
orator*, nine in *On the state*, whereas subsequently the maximum is
five. This enables Cicero to evoke varied intellectual communities.
In both dialogues there is a mixture of generations. In *On the orator*,
the two protagonists, Crassus and Antonius, are in their late forties
or early fifties, recent holders of the consulship and at the peak of
their powers; Catulus, also a consular, is a few years older. Scaevola,
Crassus' father-in-law and twenty years his senior, represents an
earlier generation – and through his connection with Scipio Aemilianus, as the son-in-law of Scipio's great friend Laelius, pushes the
sense of connection back even further. And the remaining three
characters, Caesar Strabo (Catulus' half-brother), Cotta, and
Sulpicius Rufus, are all in their thirties, members of the Senate but
still aspirants towards the highest offices. Similarly, in *On the state*,
the central characters of Scipio Aemilianus and Laelius are sur-
rounded by a group of friends of varied ages but united by their
participation in public life. L. Furius Philus and Sp. Mummius are
near-contemporaries; M'. Manilius represents an older generation;
and the remaining four are Laelius' two sons-in-law, C. Fannius and

109

Q. Mucius Scaevola, who also appears in *On the orator*, Scipio's nephew Q. Aelius Tubero and, finally, the youngest of the group, P. Rutilius Rufus who had served under Scipio in Spain.

By using a wide range of interlocutors Cicero is evoking a particular ideal of intellectual discussion, one in which a group of friends gather spontaneously and a serious discussion arises naturally from matters of current concern. There are connections of blood and marriage between some of the participants, but friendship is the dominant bond; and all participants are Roman politicians. The mingling of ages makes the conversations a means of transmitting knowledge and opinions to younger generations, and thus embodies the Roman ideal of learning how to be a politician by shadowing one's seniors. The conversation in *On the orator* starts with Crassus saying that he does not need to encourage Cotta and Sulpicius as orators, since they are already highly skilled and at the head of their generation;[89] and in *On the state* Laelius turns the discussion from natural phenomena to political disturbances by exhorting the *adulescentes* to consider ways of healing the split in the state.[90] The conversations these texts represent are didactic, and experience is teaching youth.

The didacticism is not restricted to the dramatic portrayal. To some extent, Cicero is attempting to teach his readers; but he is also himself a part of the conversations he reports. The key here is the way that Cicero explains how he knows what was said at meetings at which he was not himself present. He explains that he was told about the conversations in *On the orator* by Cotta;[91] and at the opening of book 2 he fleshes out his own authority by reminding the reader both of his family connections with the two men (his uncle by marriage Gaius Aculeo was a close friend of Crassus, and his uncle L. Cicero served under Antonius during the latter's Cilician command) and that he himself spent time at Crassus' house.[92] He claims his knowledge of the conversation in *On the state* comes from P. Rutilius Rufus, whom he met in Smyrna in the early 70s BC. The latter is clearly a more tenuous connection, but it is not impossible; and the apparent plausibility of the frame is supported by Cicero's care in getting his historical details right. Both treatises record an event which *could* have happened: all the people involved could have gathered at the specified time and place.

The communities described in these works are ones to which Cicero himself in some sense belongs. Although he was not present at either conversation he is a part of them because he is in a position to retell them to others: through the treatises he becomes an element in an unbroken chain of acquaintance and reminiscence stretching back eighty years, and whose continuing life he is ensuring by making a written record. Moreover, the two groups of interlocutors are also linked by the figure of Scaevola, who appears in both.

Cicero never again used such a large cast of characters. Nor did he again record conversations at which he had not been present until 44 BC, towards the end of the series of philosophical works, when he used this method for the two short ethical works on old age and on friendship. Even though there are good reasons for not treating them as a pair,[93] their shared use of a historical framework is worth noting. In both works, the eponymous figure is the main character: Cato the elder's interlocutors are Scipio Aemilianus and Laelius, and Laelius himself discusses friendship with his sons-in-law Scaevola and Fannius. Cicero has, then, returned to the same circles as in *On the orator* and *On the state* for his characters: Cato the elder is in fact the only new figure to be introduced.

There is an interesting difference, however, in the framing of the conversations. Cicero knows what Laelius said on friendship because Scaevola told it to him; the frame confirms Cicero's own place within this network, and the work begins with Cicero's reminiscence of how his father introduced him as an adolescent to Scaevola and his subsequent enthusiasm for the old man's company. Moreover, the prompt for Scaevola's own reminiscence of Laelius was the quarrel between Publius Sulpicius and the then consul, Q. Pompeius; not only does this date Scaevola's reminiscence to 88 but it also takes us back to the circle of *On the orator*. But no such genealogy of conversation is in place in *Cato on old age*. Cicero explains to Atticus (here, for the only time, the dedicatee) that he wanted to write something on old age and that Atticus, on whom also old age is now a burden, seemed an appropriate dedicatee.[94] He then says, 'I have ascribed the whole conversation ... to the elder Marcus Cato, so that the discussion may have greater force; and I have put Laelius and Scipio with him, wondering that he can bear old age so easily, and I have made him reply to their questions. And if he seems to discuss things in a rather more learned way than in his books, ascribe it to Greek literature, which, it is agreed, he studied with alacrity in old age.'[95] In this dialogue, then, Cicero makes no real attempt to conceal that the work is an imaginative reconstruction, indeed drawing attention to its fictionality by obliquely admitting that his Cato is improbably learned.[96]

In the four other dialogues with a historical setting, Cicero is himself a character. The settings and personnel vary considerably. In the lost *Hortensius*, the setting was Lucullus' villa and the characters Lucullus, Hortensius, Catulus and Cicero; on the basis of the surviving fragments, it can be dated only to the period between Lucullus' return to Italy in 66 and the death of Catulus in 61 or 60. The first edition of the *Academica* used the same characters, and the setting was Hortensius' villa, at some point between Cicero's consulship and the death of Catulus. *On the nature of the gods* is set much earlier, in 76, and the characters are Cotta, Gaius Velleius and Quintus Lucilius Balbus, with Cicero as a silent auditor. The organisation of *On ends* is more complex: the first two books are set in 50, and Cicero's interlocutors are Lucius Torquatus and Gaius Triarius; the conversation in books 3 and 4 is presented as the result of a chance meeting between Cicero and Marcus Cato in the library of Lucullus' son in 52; and the final book is back in 79 BC, with a larger cast: Cicero, his cousin Lucius and brother Quintus, Atticus, and Marcus Pupius Piso.

What sorts of communities are these? There are two different impulses at work. Initially, as Cicero began his ambitious philosophical programme in 46, he turned to the core of the optimates at the time of his consulship: Catulus, Lucullus and Hortensius. He put himself back to the time of his greatest political success and influence, and into a group of men with whose views he had ultimately sided – and which had now been so comprehensively overturned by Caesar. The *mise-en-scène* of the first philosophical dialogues can, then, be seen as representing Cicero's desire for the lost republic. But as characters in a plausible philosophical dialogue this group of men is less successful, inasmuch as their ignorance of philosophy undermines the verisimilitude; and while Cicero appears to have found them satisfactory as the speakers in *Hortensius*, an introductory work, he rapidly found it unworkable for the dense epistemology of the *Academica*: hence the second edition with more philosophically competent interlocutors. And we can trace the desire for verisimilitude in the subsequent historical settings, where the characters Cicero chooses did, it seems, possess enough knowledge to play their parts credibly. Indeed, some of his interlocutors are otherwise relatively obscure: so, for example, are Velleius and Balbus in *On the nature of the gods*, or Triarius in *On ends*. Their knowledge of philosophy is an important element in why Cicero chose to portray them.

Nonetheless, suitability is not the only factor. If all Cicero had wished to do was expound philosophical doctrines, then he could have adopted throughout the format of *On duties* and imparted the material as an unbroken exposition in his own voice. Two threads can be discerned. One is an elegiac evocation of those recently dead on the Republican side in the civil war: so the younger Cato and Torquatus, who died at Thapsus. I return to this in Chapter 4. The other is the demonstration of Cicero's lifelong commitment to philosophy and also the length of time that Romans have been philosophically aware: which gets particular emphasis in the final book of *On ends*, where the young Romans discuss philosophy in a city whose native philosophical traditions have recently been uprooted by the Romans. One reading of this would be as a symbolic display that philosophy has also been transmitted by conquest from Athens to Rome.

The settings of the dialogues, despite their variety, can thus be seen to fall into two distinct categories. There are the dialogues set in the past where the characters, with the exception of Cicero himself (and Atticus and Quintus in the fifth book of *On ends*) are dead at the time of writing; and there are dialogues with a contemporary setting and a very restricted range of speakers. The initial impulse behind this, in the three dialogues written before the civil war, may have been the desire to insert Cicero and his circle into a historical sequence of distinguished statesmen discussing political issues at a

113

time of crisis: Scipio Aemilianus in 129, Lucius Crassus in 91, and Cicero in 52. And, for all their atmosphere of imminent peril, it remains possible to read these three as serious reflections upon the scope and possibilities of political action. But with the dialogues written after the civil war the two categories underscore the narrowing of opportunity: either one must look to the past, or to a very restricted present.

It is important to see that Cicero's practice here does represent choices: had he desired to use a wide range of characters in a contemporary setting, he could have done so. The impression, that is, of narrowed intellectual horizons during Caesar's dictatorship is, arguably, false: the forties were a period of considerable and exciting literary activity of which Cicero was very much a part. But he has chosen in his own works from this period to place widespread creativity and discussion firmly in the past.

Written texts thus play a key part in articulating and maintaining those networks of relationships which were essential to a public career. And Cicero extends the scope of his textual relationships beyond his dealings with his contemporaries through speeches and letters to include the creation of an intellectual community, and history, in his treatises. The fictional communities of the treatises are also a response to the unsatisfactory nature of his life under Caesar; and in the next chapter I shall turn to consider more widely the ways in which Cicero's writings interact with the occasions when his public activities were not successful.

4

Failure

Previous chapters have in general taken a sympathetic view of the relationship between Cicero's writings and the other manifestations of his public career: writing is an element in his success, and there is a good fit between his intentions as a writer and the effects of his writings. But as an overall assessment of Cicero it is arguable that this is too rosy a picture: Cicero's actions, at least as a public figure, could be seen ultimately not to have achieved their ends, and his failures demonstrate either that the brilliance of his writings was an irrelevance, or that they were in fact not as effective as their subsequent critical reputation – with the exception of his poetry – would suggest.

It is not my intention to engage directly with the question of how to pronounce judgement on Cicero: quite apart from the general validity of the question, any answer must be grounded in a survey of late Republican history which is beyond the scope of this book. But there are important questions to address about Cicero's own handling of failure and about the articulation of his responses to failure in texts. I have already explored in Chapter 2 the methods whereby Cicero attempts to cope with the consequences of his exile: a palpable failure as a public figure which can nonetheless be rewritten to accord with Cicero's preferred self-image, and indeed enhance it. In this chapter I shall consider first a striking example of writing and failure in the pre-civil war period, before turning to Cicero's response to Caesar's dictatorship and its aftermath. In each case Cicero used writing to impose a form of success upon a situation which was, actually or potentially, one of failure.

Failure and competition: silencing the past

If competition was at the heart of Roman public life, then failure was an inevitable part of the political scene. Elections could be lost, jurors could vote for the other side, and the Senate or people could refuse their support for particular measures. And each of these places of potential defeat corresponded to an opportunity, or necessity, to speak. Forensic and deliberative oratory, in other words, was always delivered in contexts in which the audience might withhold their assent. As a public figure who had structured his career around oratory, Cicero was thus always potentially vulnerable to situations in which his skills were demonstrated to be ineffective.

That, at least, was the situation concerning spoken oratory. Writing brought with it the opportunity to edit the past: and I have considered in Chapter 1 the nature of the fit between what Cicero said in public and what he chose to record. And written versions also sidestep the issue of failure inasmuch as they do not indicate the verdict. Indeed, since they purport to be a record of what was said during the trial, thus obviously before the jurors came to a decision, they cannot know the future. Readers will only be able to judge the speech against its outcome if they can bring that knowledge to the speech from some other source.

The factors which influenced Cicero in deciding whether or not to produce a written version of a particular speech changed over time, but one remarkably constant element is that his written corpus largely excludes forensic speeches which ended in failure: two examples only are positively attested, though there are a number where the verdict is not known. The more striking of the two is the written defence of Milo, inasmuch as it comes late in Cicero's career, and so the motive for dissemination which may have been relevant earlier, that is simply to get his name and skills known whenever possible, since opportunities were limited, is not plausible. Why should a senior consular preserve the record of a failure?

As it happens, we know a great deal about the circumstances of the case, largely from Asconius' commentary on the speech. The unusual depth of background material makes it possible to consider why Cicero might break so abruptly with his habits and record, for posterity, a failure.

Milo was on trial as a result of the death of Clodius on the Appian Way in a brawl on 18 January 52. The trial, which took place in early April, was held under a new law on violence which had been rushed through in the aftermath of Clodius' death and the rioting which followed it; this law reduced the amount of time available to the advocates and reversed the order of events, so that evidence was now presented before the speeches. Moreover, the trial itself was disrupted by Clodius' supporters, and after the first day an armed guard was posted in the forum. It was generally thought that Pompeius, who was now sole consul and had overseen the new violence law, wished to see Milo convicted. Cicero's decision to defend Milo, therefore, placed him at the centre of a fraught political stand-off and was arguably his first challenge to Pompeius since being brought back into line after the conference of Luca; equally, not defending Milo would have compounded the manifest futility and weakness of Cicero's public activities since May 56. No one questioned the fact that Milo, who had been a firm supporter of Cicero since his tribunate in 57, had been responsible for the death of Clodius: for Cicero not to have defended the man who removed his enemy would have been an extraordinary abandonment of duty and obligation, which in turn would have indicated an extraordinary degree of weakness.

However, the trial does not seem to have been a great professional success. Milo was convicted; and a tradition grew up that Cicero's own performance had been below his normal standards. The critical accounts in Plutarch and Dio of Cicero's panic and its effect on his speaking need not be believed, but Asconius records that the supporters of Clodius shouted during Cicero's speech and as a result he did not speak with his normal 'resolution'.[1] Also according to Asconius, a version of what Cicero said at the trial was written down and subsequently circulated. This version survived to the time of Quintilian, at least, but was subsequently lost: our *On behalf of Milo*, a different speech, was circulated by Cicero at some point after the trial.[2] It is not known how or why the speech which Cicero delivered at the trial was recorded. It is unclear whether the techniques of shorthand then current were effective enough to have secured a verbatim record or whether what was recorded was simply a summary; and it is also impossible to know whether the motive for preserving a record of Cicero's speech was curiosity and interest in a major public event, or whether there was a desire to embarrass Cicero. Indeed, it is possible that the first *On behalf of Milo* should be placed within the boundaries of forgery, permeable and ill-defined as questions of authorship were in the ancient world. At any rate, Asconius' story does not suggest that Cicero had anything to do with the circulation of the first version, and that would imply that someone else exercised some form of editorial role. The relevance of this episode to the general problem of the relationship between Cicero's spoken and written speeches has quite rightly been dismissed; but it does have a bearing on Cicero's practice in *disseminating* written versions of his speeches.

The existence of the first *On behalf of Milo* meant the aftermath of Milo's trial was different from the circumstances which Cicero normally faced after a defeat. Attempting to bury the case in oblivion was not an option, since an unauthorised version was, almost certainly, already in circulation.[3] Not only did this version keep the fact of the trial and verdict alive, but it also memorialised an unsatisfactory record of Cicero's skills. Indeed, it is possible that the story of Cicero's loss of nerve arose because the first written version of *On behalf of Milo*, the one now lost, was, in comparison with the style of Cicero's other written speeches, awkward and abrupt: not because he delivered it incompetently but because the transcription of an oral delivery would inevitably appear rough and unpolished in comparison with a written presentation.[4]

The initial impulse to publish *On behalf of Milo* may, then, have been the desire to supersede the unsatisfactory pirated version. Cicero's reputation as an orator appears to have been under attack on stylistic grounds during these years, and he had also recently suffered a number of embarrassing defeats: good grounds for his not being confident enough to leave the transcription unchallenged.[5] But at least two further considerations can be adduced.

One is that the trial of Milo was not the end of the story. The judicial consequences of Clodius' death continued into 51 as other men who had been involved either in his murder or in the rioting were tried, and Cicero continued to act as advocate. In the immediate aftermath of Milo's conviction, Milo's assistant Saufeius, who had actually supervised Clodius' death, was tried twice: on both occasions Cicero was one of his advocates and on both occasions he was acquitted. Numerous of Clodius' supporters were also tried over the summer of 52, though Cicero was not directly involved in their trials; but after 10 December, when the tribunes of the year left office and became liable for prosecution, Cicero did, most unusually, take on a prosecution against Munatius Plancus Bursa, who had been a consistent supporter of Clodius. This was the first time Cicero had undertaken a prosecution since that of Verres in 70, and Bursa was convicted. In describing Bursa's conviction in a letter, Cicero relates it back to the trial of Milo;[6] and if all this judicial activity was perceived as being connected, then it would still be valuable to promote an interpretation which was hostile to Clodius and favourable to Milo even after Milo's conviction, since it might affect the outcomes of the other trials which were still going on.

A second consideration is the interest in the trial of Milo itself. Asconius records that Marcus Brutus disagreed with the defence strategy that Cicero adopted, and after the verdict wrote his own speech. In it he used the public interest defence: that is, he did not attempt to deny that Milo had had Clodius killed, but had argued that this was justified in the interests of the state. It remains unclear how far Brutus believed that this might have been effective at the trial itself, and how far he was using the occurrence of the trial as an opportunity to comment upon the political situation: either way, the existence of this text could easily be read as a reproach to Cicero's failure. Cicero's surviving version does incorporate the public interest defence: and one of the major critical difficulties with this speech lies in this inconsistency, claiming both that Milo did not kill Clodius but that, if he had done, it would have been justified. Whether it be read as a rebuke to Brutus (by demonstrating how such a defence should be used) or as a compliment to his insight remains as a problem, but that Brutus' version was invoked, at least implicitly, in Cicero's second thoughts is highly likely.

Where, then, does this leave the surviving version of *On behalf of*

Milo? One major interpretative problem is the extent of knowledge that Cicero expected his readers to bring to the text. He had written 'fictional' speeches before: that is, in relation to the trial of Verres he had had disseminated, in a form that matched the conventions of written speeches, the text of a speech which had never been delivered. Brutus' *On behalf of Milo* presumably gave the impression of being a real speech. But arguably these are not an exact match to the circumstances of the second *On behalf of Milo*. In this speech, Cicero is not simply promulgating a text of a speech that was never delivered. He is disseminating the text which purports to be the speech which he gave on a particular occasion when Cicero did, in fact, deliver a speech – just not this one. There is the opportunity here for a greater degree of deception than in the *Verrines*, or Brutus' *On behalf of Milo*. And we know that the attribution of authorship was sufficiently fluid in the late Republic for Cicero to hope that, with Atticus' aid, he might be able to claim that the speech *Against Clodius and Curio*, full of injudicious vitriol, was in fact a forgery.[7] It is entirely possible, I would suggest, that Cicero's ultimate intention was for his written version to replace the pirate version, as the speech which was actually delivered on 7 April 52. This would not change the known verdict at the trial, but the improved speech might preserve Cicero in a more favourable light than the pirated version appears to have done.

However, Cicero had to account for the possibility that there were readers who would already be in possession of the pirated version – not to mention Brutus' attempt – and who might also have been present at the trial, and who would read his official account with this background in mind. Many of the critical problems that this speech poses can in fact be addressed by taking the variety of the audiences into account, since the speech has two roles: both to be an entirely convincing defence of Milo which could have been delivered at the trial, and a response to those readers who knew that it was not the speech delivered at the trial.

As far as the former audience is concerned, the existence of the revised *On behalf of Milo* is in itself a sufficient response to the failure at the trial: Cicero might have preferred to allow the affair to be forgotten, but since that appeared to be impossible, he could at least attempt to ensure that the record of the trial displayed his oratorical skills to advantage. More complex, however, is the manipulation of failure evident once one considers *On behalf of Milo* in relation to a more knowledgeable audience.

The opening paragraphs appear to create the impression of being present in the forum, with their description of what Cicero can see; but they also refer to the feelings of anxiety which these sights cause in him. Cicero here is making a record of an unprecedented judicial occasion which saw armed force present in the city legitimated by and at the behest of an *imperium*-wielding magistrate. But if a rumour had got around that Cicero had been terrified at Milo's trial, then the opening is also a response: a confession that he had felt fear, but an explanation for this not in terms of personal cowardice, but of alarm at the break with civilian tradition.[8] And although there are references to Milo's appearance (§92) there are also hints that Milo himself is not available: there is the reference to his 'voices' in §93, which is an oddly disembodied way for Milo to communicate with Cicero. But although the speech inevitably reads differently if one brings to it knowledge of the verdict, it is not concerned, at least not concerned for its own sake, with drawing attention to its fictionality. The interaction with a knowing audience deals more with moulding the recollection of the death of Clodius and the trial and conviction of Milo.

The narrative which Cicero tells has a number of components. In the first place, there is the figure of Milo. Although there is nothing in the speech which conflicts with its purported time and place of delivery, the characterisation of Milo is so constructed that the fact of his conviction can become part of the heroic myth. He 'has been born to this fate, that he cannot even save himself without saving also you and the state with him'.[9] The death of Clodius is of benefit to all – a fundamental premise in the speech; and if Milo is convicted as the perpetrator of this act, he can console himself with the knowledge of what he has achieved.[10] This reflection is supported by Cicero's likening of Milo to five other Romans who had had men killed and whose actions, at least on a conservative reading of the constitutional position, were legitimate; and while the main aim here must be to insert Milo into a specific canon of great Romans, brief reflection would indicate that most of the men on his list had also suffered as a result of what they did, whatever their ultimate rehabilitation.[11] The possibility of failure, as represented by judicial conviction, is now a hideous threat to men who have entered public life with the highest of motives:

> What can be imagined or stated that is more demanding, more worrying, or more trying for us two, who have entered public life in the hope of the greatest of rewards but are not free from the fear of the most cruel punishments? While I had always thought Milo would have to face other storms and squalls in the rough sea of public meetings, since he always was in accord with good men against the wicked, I never expected, in the law court itself and in the council where the most respectable men out of all the orders made up their minds, that Milo's enemies would have a hope not only of ending his safety but also of destroying his glory through such men.[12]

Nonetheless, Cicero is also concerned to stress that Milo's reputation will survive whatever happens:

> He [sc. Milo] adds, which is certainly true, that brave and wise men are accustomed not so much to seek the rewards of right actions but the right actions themselves; and that he has done nothing during his life which is not highly distinguished, provided that nothing is more outstanding for a man than to free his country from danger. He says that those men are blessed for whom such an act is a source of honour from their fellow citizens, but still those whose services towards their fellow citizens are greater than what they have received in return are not unhappy. Nonetheless, of all the rewards of virtue – if we must compare rewards – the most substantial is the reward of glory; this is the one thing which soothes the shortness of life by the memory of generations to come, and which allows us to be present when absent and to live when dead.[13]

Here the possibility of self-referential reading is most enticing, since

Milo is already absent, and already continuing his existence through the preservation of his glorious memory. And by sending this speech to Milo in Massilia Cicero was seeking to act out this consolation by reassuring Milo that he was not forgotten; indeed, that his actions were preserved in a magnificent piece of writing. It was, after all, always possible that Milo might, at some point in the future, be able to return to Rome.

Opposing the taciturn, unwavering and self-sacrificing Milo is the figure of Clodius. This is of course far from the first time that Cicero attacked Clodius in writing – though the invective of §§72-91 is notable both for its scope and polish. But what is new about *On behalf of Milo* is that, this time, there would be no comeback. It was the one piece of invective to which Cicero could be sure that Clodius would not respond. The speech *On behalf of Milo* is not simply a gift for Milo; it is also Cicero's opportunity to impose textual closure on Clodius. By having disseminated a version of *On behalf of Milo* which includes such a comprehensive and devastating portrait of Clodius, Cicero was attempting to fix him for posterity as a sacrilegious monster whose continued existence was incompatible with that of Rome. And it is possible that this characterisation of Clodius was something which Cicero had not included in the original speech at the trial, or not included in this form: quite apart from the difficulties of reconciling the *extra causam* section, in which most of the invective against Clodius appears, with the rest of the speech in terms of its rhetorical and legal form, it would surely have been unappealing to attack Clodius in this way when his supporters were present with menacing attitudes.

The central figures of Clodius and Milo are supported by two further characters: Pompeius and Cicero himself. Cicero faced two problems in handling Pompeius in this speech. One was that Pompeius was acting in a way that strongly suggested he wanted Milo's conviction. But Cicero was not in a position where he could attempt to defuse the jurors' perception of Pompeius' hostility by a straightforward attack on Pompeius' authority and actions. His second problem was that Pompeius' stance appears to have been generally popular. He had no difficulty in getting senatorial support for his legislation on violence, and the very fact of his nomination as sole consul suggests that the political classes at Rome wanted, above all, an end to violence and a return to constitutional decorum. Cicero's response is to demonstrate his support for Pompeius in general while denying that Pompeius' recent actions have been an attack on Milo. He does so by characterising Pompeius' public actions since Clodius' death as ones concerned with the order and safety of the state, rather than as directed against Milo; and since, on Cicero's telling, Milo too is concerned only with the order and safety of the state, Pompeius cannot have been intending Milo harm. So an opposition is set up between military force and the judgements of the courts: since Pompeius has chosen not to take direct military activity against Milo, but refer the matter to the courts, it is clear that he has not prejudged the issue.[14] Insofar as the soldiers in the forum are relevant, it is as protectors of due procedure.[15] And Cicero even suggests that one of Pompeius' motives has been to appear even-handed, given that Milo was his friend, and Clodius his enemy.[16]

Cicero, then, gives Pompeius an important role in the speech, and does not attempt to conceal Pompeius' part in the sequence of events which have led up to the trial. And from §67 onwards he gives Pompeius such detailed prominence that some interpreters of the speech have argued that the final part of the speech is hostile to Pompeius and therefore – since the earlier part of the speech is favourable – it must be a later addition. That is, the alleged inconsistency in Cicero's attitude to Pompeius marks the existence of revisions in the preparation of the text for dissemination.[17]

This is an interesting argument, but we need to be careful in determining exactly what is meant by hostility to Pompeius. There is certainly no open attack; indeed, Pompeius is treated with apparent courtesy, and those who see the last part of the speech as fundamentally anti-Pompeius make frequent recourse to the concept of irony. Moreover, it remains to be asked why Cicero put into circulation a speech containing this inconsistency. The further from the actual date of the trial one wishes to posit dissemination, the more difficult it becomes to argue that any perceived inconsistencies are an oversight on Cicero's part due to haste in composition. It could of course be that Cicero is constructing a speech which is deliberately inconsistent precisely in order to draw attention to a particular issue – in

4. Failure

this case, the behaviour of Pompeius – but it becomes more difficult to maintain this if, as is the case in *On behalf of Milo*, the existence of inconsistency is itself a matter for debate.

I would suggest, rather, that the characterisation of Pompeius in *On behalf of Milo* is, in part, another example of memorialisation. That is, one of Cicero's aims is to record in a permanent form what Pompeius did in the first half of 52 BC: to prevent his actions from being forgotten. Insofar, then, as Pompeius did things during this period which were of questionable constitutional propriety, Cicero leaves open the possibility for his reader to form a hostile picture of Pompeius. But it is impossible, I think, to point to any passage in which Cicero says something directly critical of Pompeius.

Cicero begins his handling of Pompeius, at §65, thus:

> I praised the unbelievable carefulness of Gnaeus Pompeius, but I shall say what I feel. Those to whom the whole state is entrusted are forced to hear too many things, nor can they do otherwise.[18]

There are three points here. One is the compliment to Pompeius. The second is Cicero's claim to unfettered speech. And the third is the generalising statement describing Pompeius' position within the state, that is as the man to whom the state has been entrusted. Cicero goes on to pick out three incidents where Pompeius responded to an apparent threat: an alleged conspiracy among Milo's slaves to murder him; an attack on Julius Caesar's house; and an allegation in the Senate that Milo was carrying a weapon. There is a twofold point being made in the paragraph which follows: that what Pompeius has displayed on each of these occasions is caution, not fear; and that the fact that in each case the threat proved not to be substantiated shows that Pompeius' showing concern about events is not proof that there is any reason for his concern. That is, even if Pompeius were to be suspicious of Milo, that would not prove that his suspicions were well-grounded.

Cicero goes on to address Pompeius directly, confessing to Milo's fears that he is the object of suspicion to Pompeius. But he undermines this scenario from various directions. He describes all of

Pompeius' military forces, and expresses astonishment that they could all be directed at a single individual. But he then corrects that assumption: the point of these forces is to restore order, and in that enterprise Milo is at one with Pompeius. And Cicero concludes the address to Pompeius with reflections on the mutability of fortune and the value of true friends. He then turns to the jury and picks up on the arguments made earlier in the speech, that the show of force has not determined the outcome of the trial, but is in place merely to ensure the safety of their deliberations.

This passage, addressed to Pompeius and then to the jurors, is the bridge passage to the final part of the speech, in which Cicero uses the argument that Clodius deserved to die and that, even had Milo killed him, he would have been justified in the killing. Pompeius occurs in this argument as one of Clodius' victims, and as someone who would not summon Clodius back from the underworld, even if that were possible; and there are allusions to the friendship between Clodius and Pompeius.[19] Pompeius does not appear in a heroic light here: he was shut up in his house by Clodius' gangs, and did not take steps to oppose Clodius. But Cicero is careful to modify the force of any criticism: Pompeius is described in this final section of the speech as 'an exceptionally brave and glorious citizen', 'an outstanding consul', as someone 'whose ability and good fortune have been such as to enable him to achieve what no one else can', and as 'the very man who could have resisted Clodius'. It may also be worth noting that Cicero avoids naming Pompeius in a number of these places, and this may in part be to put space between the Pompeius of the time of publication and the man who, along with everyone else except Milo, was, on Cicero's telling of events, unable to resist Clodius.

What is Cicero trying to achieve in this portrayal of Pompeius? The focus in the speech is on the relationship between him and Milo, and its contrast with his attitude towards Clodius; but to a certain extent this is a smokescreen. With Milo now in exile, Pompeius' favour was of less immediate moment to him. But the characterisation also makes sense within the broader narrative Cicero is seeking to enshrine in this speech. Cicero's problem, as he came to rewrite *On behalf of Milo*, was not simply the desire to efface an unsuccessful performance and influence subsequent judicial events –

the factors which I discussed above. He had some explaining of his own to do. What had he been doing, with so close a relationship to a character like Milo? And Milo's reputation for violence did not evaporate with Clodius' death. In addition to the incidents which Cicero recounts – the assassination plot by Milo's gladiators, the allegation that he entered the Senate house with a dagger – Asconius lists further allegations, including kidnap and the unauthorised torture of slaves in Clodius' household.[20] Moreover, he records that most people assumed that Milo had chosen to go into exile immediately after Clodius' death, and were surprised by his return to Rome; and that Milo immediately stepped up his campaign for the consulship with extensive bribery.[21] It is easy to see why Milo had become very unpopular with large numbers of Romans, and that many would not have regretted his conviction. Given that this was the case, Cicero needs to produce a different narrative which puts Milo in a good light, and replaces the brutal thug with his train of gladiators and his lavish purse by a brave and devoted patriot. And he needs to do this less for Milo's sake than for his own: to rescue his reputation not simply from oratorical failure but also from a highly dubious friendship. Having decided not simply to abandon Milo to oblivion after the verdict, major restructuring is required.

Pompeius is important in this task because his reputation can be made to guarantee Milo's. He is the protector of Rome; and if he sees no threat in Milo, then Milo is vindicated. §§67-71 act out, for the jurors, the process of convincing Pompeius that Milo is, even if not innocent – and the actual death of Clodius is not the focus of this section – at least no threat either to Pompeius or to Rome. Cicero faced a huge challenge in attempting to do this, because Pompeius' actions since the death of Clodius *had* demonstrated sustained suspicion of Milo: not simply in the nature of the special legislation under which Milo was tried but also through his public manifestations of fear, secluding himself in his villa and on one occasion breaking off a meeting of the Senate 'saying that he was afraid of Milo's arrival'.[22] Asconius, who preserves this detail, introduces it by saying, 'Pompeius was afraid of Milo, or pretended that he was afraid'; and the suggestion, whatever it is based on, that we have here an example of Pompeius' famed *dissimulatio*, is attractive. It was clearly in Pompeius' interests to maintain the impression of being under threat if he was to justify his vigorous measures to restore order, and even genuine fear about his safety could be combined with a self-conscious performance of that fear.

Cicero's attempt to rehabilitate Milo takes account of this background. He cannot ignore Pompeius' apparent attitude to Milo: hence the detail in this speech about Pompeius' past actions, which Stone sees as criticism of him. It is possible for a supporter of Milo to read this passage as hostile towards Pompeius because it recalls the importance of Pompeius' actions in the sequence of events which led to Milo's exile; but I would suggest that Cicero's main aim is not criticism of Pompeius *per se*, but rather to demonstrate that his suspicions of Milo were unfounded, and that Milo does not bear any grudge as a result – hence the statement, relying on the evocation of the time before the verdict, that Milo would leave Rome 'without hesitation' if that was the only way to preserve peace. Cicero then proceeds to imagine Milo telling Pompeius that a time might come when he would value loyal friends. This is potentially double-edged: does Milo mean that he will always be faithful to Pompeius, even if exiled, or is it rather a reminder to Pompeius that, by allowing the conviction of Milo, he will lose a friend who might be valuable in changed circumstances? The movement of thought in the passage, with its stress of Milo's reliability and self-sacrifice, would point to the former, but the latter cannot be ruled out, and the ambiguity encourages the reader to reflect on Pompeius' behaviour. Cicero is not letting Pompeius completely off the hook: he needs to demonstrate that his own commitment to Milo was justified. But this passage can be also be taken is imposing closure on the case of Milo. Milo will accept his fate: it is possible, therefore, to move on.

I have already remarked that the characterisation of Milo in *On behalf of Milo* is more for Cicero's benefit than for Milo's, and it remains to consider Cicero's presentation of himself in the speech. Unsurprisingly, he is hostile to Clodius and supportive of Milo; and one could read the device of saying what Milo would say as a reflection on the situation when Cicero wrote this second version: given that Milo is now in exile, he can now speak only through others.[23] But Cicero also emphasises that he is close to Pompeius:

indeed, one of the claims that Milo has on Pompeius' goodwill is that he has been a supporter of Cicero. So, for example, 'he would prove to you ... that his tribunate was, under your guidance, directed at my safety, which has always been very dear to you.'[24] So, Cicero refers to being among the first to be summoned when a plot to assassinate Pompeius was thought to be discovered among Milo's slaves: a senior position in Pompeius' *consilium* is a clear marker of his status.[25] On Cicero's account, he, Pompeius and Milo all belong to a self-reinforcing network of benevolence and loyalty. It is certainly possible to interpret this narrative as one which is critical of Pompeius, given his undeniable role in Milo's conviction; but I do not think it necessary to believe that Cicero intended the speech as an attack on Pompeius. As I have discussed, reference to what Pompeius did is inevitable if Cicero is to rehabilitate his own relationship with Milo. Indeed, it could be argued that the stress in the speech on the jurors' freedom to decide – that the forces in the forum are there for protection and not intimidation – is in fact a tribute to Pompeius and to his skill in reintroducing order and returning Rome to its normal constitutional position.

Such a view also illuminates the end of the speech. The final chapters are an increasingly emotional appeal to the jurors' feelings through a description of the unwavering Milo as he prepares to face exile, which concludes with, 'But let there be an end; I can no longer speak for tears, and Milo has forbidden tears in his defence.'[26] But this is not quite the end.[27] The final sentences are:

> I beg and beseech you, gentlemen of the jury, that when you vote you dare to express what you feel. Believe me, your bravery, justice and honesty will particularly be approved of by the man who in choosing jurors chose the best and wisest and most courageous.[28]

A final appeal to the jurors' courage and a reassurance that they can vote as they wish: but, for the readers of this revised version, who know that there is now no jury, this is a confirmation by Cicero of his belief that Pompeius was impartial, despite Milo's conviction. Moreover, it is important to remind readers of the existence of a jury, since Cicero's narrative of events demands that the jurors be mistaken. If Milo is innocent, and Pompeius is not attempting to interfere with the course of justice, then the only explanation for the outcome is that the jurors got it wrong. In a speech which purports to have been delivered before the voting, this sentiment can nowhere be made explicit. But it is the conclusion which Cicero needs the knowing readers of the revised version to draw on their own.

On behalf of Milo is, then, a narrative of exoneration. Cicero is not at fault; Pompeius is not at fault; Milo is not at fault. Clodius is the solitary figure of evil, and with his death the threat to the state has evaporated to the relief of all, demonstrated most strikingly in the thought-experiment of bringing Clodius back from the dead (79). And since the speech purports to be prior to the verdict, the actual process whereby the jurors did convict Milo can be left untouched. Milo famously is said to have remarked, on receiving his copy in exile, that it was as well that Cicero had not delivered this speech: had he done so, he, Milo, would not be enjoying the mullets of Massilia.[29] Whether Milo intended this as a compliment to Cicero's skills or, as Dio himself suggests, it was bitter, has been debated. But it is generally agreed that the point of the remark is that the revised version could have secured Milo's acquittal; indeed, there has been debate about what exactly in the revised version could have accomplished this. But even if that is what Milo meant, it seems to put rather a lot of weight on a brief and witty remark. I wonder whether Milo actually meant that, had Cicero given the revised version – with its volcanic attack on Clodius – neither he, nor probably Cicero, would have left the forum alive.

At any event, I would argue that our version of *On behalf of Milo* is not simply, or indeed primarily, about showing that Cicero had the skills to defend his client successfully, even if he did not manage to secure victory on the day. This is not to say that bolstering Cicero's reputation for oratorical brilliance had no part in his decision to write this speech up. But more importantly it provided Cicero with the opportunity to take stock of what had happened and construct an account of events which would close off the story of Milo and Clodius and allow those still standing, as it were, to proceed. And arguably, what is at stake in the speech is not simply remedying the damage to the reputations of individuals. The speech also seeks to make normal and acceptable the extraordinary breaches of constitutional propriety of the first half of 52, above all those which centred upon the figure of Pompeius. He was a holder of *imperium* who operated within the city, a sole consul, and a holder of consular and pro-consular *imperium* simultaneously. Moreover, troops were now present within Rome. Cicero ignores the anomalies of Pompeius' position: nothing is to be considered as interfering with normal judicial decision-making.

On behalf of Milo is Cicero's last judicial speech: *On behalf of Ligarius* and *On behalf of King Deiotarus*, delivered during Caesar's dictatorship, belong to a very different environment even if, superficially, they might appear to be forensic. But this formulation conceals the extent to which the rules have already changed by the time of *On behalf of Milo*; and this concealment is already present in this speech's enormous effort to conceal the failure of the institutions of government and to pretend that everything is as it always has been.

The end of oratory: *Brutus* and *Orator*

In the previous chapter I considered the communities which Cicero created within his treatises and the ways in which the treatises themselves bear witness to the existence of intellectual communities through the mechanisms of dedications and, once, of supporting letter. The treatises, I suggested, enable Cicero to create for himself a genealogy for his participation in public life, since the characters in them are usually also active politicians; these groups stand for his (missing) familial heritage, and at the same time bolster his own intellectual interests by demonstrating that they have been the pastime of the elite for a century and more.

Cicero's first substantial treatises after his return to Rome in 47 were rhetorical, and thus a return to the material covered in *On the orator*; and it is worth speculating how far Cicero expected their rather different approach to speaking to be read against his earlier reflections. They also formed a substantial set of overtures towards Brutus: both *Brutus* and *Orator*, along with the slighter *Paradoxes of the Stoics*, are dedicated to him, and are often read as important documents in the Atticist/ Asianist controversy, in which Cicero's style was attacked by those who advocated a lean, spare style of speaking which was explicitly modelled on the Attic orators of the fourth century, above all Lysias. As such, *Brutus* and *Orator* contribute to a narrative in which the ageing Cicero finds that his style of speaking has become unfashionable, and he attempts to reclaim his authority by engaging in a debate with one of the leading intellectual figures of the younger generations.[30]

I do not wish to dismiss entirely the significance of the Atticist/ Asianist debate, but there is a danger that it may obscure the wider problems to which Cicero's oratorical writings from this period seem to respond. *Brutus* and *Orator*, when taken together, enact the dissolution of the orator as he was portrayed in *On the orator*. *Brutus* considers the practical side of oratory with its historical survey of actual practitioners: and its conclusions are that few speakers at Rome have matched up to any rigorous definition of an *orator*, that Cicero himself, the closest epitome of the ideal orator yet seen, has been silenced by events, and that Brutus, as the sole hope for the future, cannot reach his full potential in the absence of vigorous competition.

The elegiac lament for a lost past that dominates *Brutus* is arguably undercut by its ending: *Orator*, by contrast, is for much of its length reluctant to acknowledge any historical dimension at all to the orator's task. Despite the title, it turns out to be a work primarily about style: and 'turns out' is a particularly apt description, given the reluctance and hesitation with which its subject emerges. Initially, all seems clear. 'Whether it is a more difficult and bigger thing to deny your frequent requests for the same topic, or to accomplish which you have been insistently asking for a long time, Brutus, I am uncertain.'[31] So starts the treatise, and a few lines later Brutus' inquiry is explained: 'For, given the range of variety among good orators, what is a greater matter than to judge what is the best aspect and, as it were, shape, of speaking?'[32] So it would seem that Brutus wants to know about speaking rather than speakers. But, as so often in Cicero's theoretical writing on rhetoric, this is an unstable distinction. He proceeds immediately to consider the problems involved in producing an answer: if he manages to describe *the orator* Brutus has been asking about, he is afraid that he will put off speakers because he has sketched an unattainable figure (§3). He tries to reassure people in that category that even second or third place in artistic endeavour is worth having, and then moves the discussion out of actual experience: 'As I create the ideal orator I shall shape such a figure as perhaps has never existed'[33] and he proceeds to relate his enterprise to Plato's theory of forms.

This uncertainty about the subject matter continues to shape the dialogue's progression: at times the subject is explicitly said to be the speaker, at times speech.[34] These conflicting statements of intent are often linked to an address to Brutus. Indeed, *Orator* is noticeable among Cicero's treatises for the frequency with which the dedicatee is invoked, as well as for the affection which Cicero demonstrates towards him. Nor is the prominence of Brutus as addressee solely to be explained in terms of the convention that a fresh argumentative start is accompanied by a summons to the reader, who is represented by the named dedicatee, and that the *Orator* is a work with a discursive argument. Rather, the figure of Brutus encapsulates the problems which Cicero now faces as an orator and as a writer about oratory. What is the *point* of writing about oratory? Who will read him, and why?

In *Brutus* this problem was located within a genealogy of orators whose tradition has been broken by civil war and the lack of opportunities for public speaking under Caesar. In *Orator*, the difficulty lies in Cicero's conception of his own role as a teacher. Near the middle of the work, he reaches the question of arrangement of thought in words (140) and confesses that the prospect of talking about this subject worries him, particularly as he is afraid not simply of those who normally find fault, but also people who admire him and may find it strange that someone of his achievements writes on 'the contrivance of speech'. He goes on to justify teaching rhetoric through a comparison with civil law: eloquence has always been more highly regarded as a civilian skill than civil law, and yet teaching civil law is regarded as a fine activity. Why then should those who teach how to speak be criticised (141-2)? Cicero here faces up to a widespread suspicion of teaching as an occupation for elite Romans, and to the fact that formal rhetorical training had not become part of the *tirocinium fori* in the way that attendance on jurists as they gave their decisions had. But he does not indicate why the issue has become a problem for him now: there was no such concern in *On the orator*, which also contains passages of considerable technical detail. At the time at which he was engaged on *Orator*, however, he was also practising declamation with members of Caesar's circle.[35] If Rome's greatest orator has become a teacher of rhetoric, then teaching, and didactic writing, must rise in value.

It could be argued, then, that *Orator* reflects Cicero's new status as an orator: no longer a great practitioner, but someone whose past experiences enable him to transmit verbal skills to a younger generation. This change is evident too in the narrowed scope of the subject, with its concentration on style, including a lengthy consideration of prose rhythm. There is no need to doubt Cicero's interest in these matters, nor that he felt rhythm was an aspect of his style of speaking which provided an opportunity to respond convincingly to Atticist criticisms. But the scope of oratory has narrowed. The first substantial section of the work handles the three 'types of speaking' (20-42, picked up again at 81-99) and there is extensive consideration of propriety in language (147-67). And while there is some attempt to follow the familiar divisions of rhetoric, it is marked by brevity and disruption, and a distaste for systematic exposition: 'I am not going to lay out precepts' (43); 'First of all I have described the nature of these two parts of speaking [sc. *inventio* and *dispositio*] in a brief and abbreviated way' (51); 'I would speak about this [sc. *actio*] at greater length if this were the time for teaching and if you were interested in this' (55); 'This [sc. decorum] is a huge subject, Brutus, as I'm sure you're aware, and needs another big book; but that's enough for what is being discussed' (73); 'Use both [sc. types of wit]; one is for telling a story wittily, and the other for the exchange of jokes, of which there are many kinds; but now we are covering something else][(87).[36] Paradoxically, then, at the very moment in his writing career at which Cicero appears to take on the mantle of the teaching, he is reiterating his distaste for detailed instruction.

There is a tension in *Orator*, then, between a defiant engagement with the abstruse and technical aspects of rhetoric and a reluctance to engage in systematic instruction. A similar tension can be traced in Cicero's attitude to earlier Roman orators. One of his starting points is a reference to the observation of M. Antonius (one of the chief interlocutors in *On the orator*) that he had seen many fluent speakers, but none who was entirely eloquent (18). A little later, having introduced the concept of 'kinds of speaking' he exclaims, 'Would that we were able to find an image of such an orator among Latin-speakers! It would be wonderful not to have to look for foreign examples and to be adequately equipped with home-grown ones.'[37] But this is not possible, and the next section (23-32), starting with Cicero's admiration for Demosthenes, discusses Attic writers in order to make a favourite point of Cicero's, that such a designation must cover a much wider range of writers and styles than Roman Atticists allow. And it is writers in Greek who provide the examples a little further on, when the exposition returns to the subject of different kinds of speech and the consequent variations in style (37-42) and then briefly to *actio* (56-60) and to the differences between oratory and other genres (62-8). The first part of *Orator* underlines the deficiency in Roman oratory, and Cicero refers explicitly to his attempts in *Brutus* to praise Roman practitioners while recalling that even there he had placed Demosthenes beyond all others (23). *Orator* confirms the futility of *Brutus*.

Just as in *Brutus*, Cicero himself is an important part of the story. But whereas *Brutus* dealt with his activity as a speaker, in *Orator* his writing is the focus. He frequently quotes from or refers to the texts of his speeches;[38] and on the first occasion, he excuses himself from choosing examples to illustrate his facility at different registers: 'I would pick out examples, if I did not think they were either known or that those who were interested could read them themselves'.[39] And he justifies these references both on the grounds of his talent (106) and on the scope of his productions: 'No orator – not even in leisurely Greek surroundings – has written an amount comparable to mine, and mine have this very variety which I am commending.'[40] When Cicero does refer to other written speeches in Latin, it is to consider their style: and while Carbo's address to Drusus receives his stamp of approval, albeit with a caution against too frequent use of his clausulae (213-15) he suggests corrections for phrases used by Crassus and C. Gracchus (222-5, 233-4).

It is not, then, that Cicero ignores the oratorical tradition at Rome entirely. But he handles it as a text-based rather than a performance-based tradition. Oratory has been turned into a scholarly discipline based on close reading: and to object that this is an essential part of talking about prose rhythm is merely to push the problem back a stage. Why should Cicero have chosen so recalcitrant and abstruse a topic for a treatise for Brutus? As he points out, it is a subject which no previous writer has handled at remotely comparable length (226).

It is perhaps relevant that Cicero's analysis of prose rhythm is both rather confusing and, it seems, at odds sometimes with his own practice.[41] There is undeniable ambition in seeking to develop a vocabulary and discourse for a hitherto understudied area: but his unease in the field encapsulates Cicero's problem with oratory by 46. How can he maintain his pre-eminence as an orator if he cannot practise it freely? He can write a history of oratory: but if he follows the logic of his argument to the extent of explicitly inscribing himself into the canon as the greatest Roman orator, he draws attention to his lack of influence in the present. And if he turns to his enormous and overwhelming textual presence as a topic, there is a risk not simply of demonstrating how dull and uninteresting oratory can be once it is divorced from its spoken presence, but of appearing as merely a technical instructor. In *Orator* Cicero is, in effect, initiating in Latin the literary criticism of written oratorical texts: the work's enormous subsequent influence shows how congenial a development this was to later writers, but at the same time is a marker of the profound transformation in the practice of oratory. Cicero's aspiration to delineate a statesman-orator in *On the orator* has been abandoned; if *Brutus* was the working out of the death of those hopes, *Orator* is a step towards a new form of criticism. It is not perhaps surprising that *Orator* is his last major work on rhetoric: Cicero's eventual response to the problem of the speechless orator is to map out and seize a new area of study.

The politician as philosopher

Cicero's philosophy-writing is often regarded as an escape from or a substitute for political activity. But while it is undeniable that this project is a different type of activity from speech-writing, and is in generic terms novel, it is important to define its relationship with the rest of his public career carefully. He was not engaged in philosophy to the exclusion of all other types of writing: in May 45 he was contemplating a letter of advice to Caesar, and he wrote a funeral oration about Cato's sister Porcia during the summer; in the autumn he defended King Deiotarus against charges that he had plotted against Caesar.[42] And although he seems not to have finished, or sent, the letter for Caesar, he had copies of his speech on Porcia and for Deiotarus swiftly disseminated. Moreover, his non-philosophical writing is clearly designed to maintain his position as a participant in public debates. The Deiotarus case presented itself as an opportunity to do so, but the other two were manufactured by Cicero himself.[43] And he is concerned during the summer of 45 BC at hostile comment about his continuing absence from Rome, following Tullia's death. In his exculpatory letters to Atticus, one of his defences is that he has been busy writing.[44] This is not the behaviour of a man who has withdrawn from public life. Cicero was still acutely aware of how he was perceived, and was still attempting to use writing as a means to bolster his public *persona*.[45]

The philosophical treatises themselves confirm the view that Cicero sees their composition as an aspect of, and not a substitute for, political activity. This is a recurrent theme in the prefaces to the treatises, which constantly rehearse justifications for Cicero's undertaking the task of writing philosophy. I have discussed in Chapter 2 the way in which Cicero manipulates the concept of *otium* in the treatises of the late 50s in order to underscore and control his narrative of exclusion from public life combined with a continuing commitment to the greatness of Rome. Similar themes dominate the openings of the Caesarian treatises: Cicero is employing his enforced *otium* in the service of the Roman people, and by creating a philosophical literature in Latin he will ensure that in this genre, as by now in others, Romans are no longer dependent upon Greek literature. An excellent example is the second book of *On divination*, which starts

As I considered and reflected widely and for a long time how I might serve as many people as possible, so that I should not interrupt at all my service to the state, no greater method occurred to me than to hand over to my fellow-citizens the paths of the best arts; and I think I have achieved this in a considerable number of volumes.[46]

This is followed by a checklist of what he had already written, and then an apology for the fact that his rate of progress is likely now to slow down, given the occurrence of 'a rather serious event' – the assassination of Caesar – and that he is now once more being involved in discussions about the state. There are now other ways of fulfilling his public duties.

The preface to book 2 of *On divination* is unusual in being very clearly tied to the context of writing and to direct and specific interaction between Cicero's philosophical writing and events in the wider world, and it is possible that Cicero wanted to dramatise the breaking news of Caesar's death and his hopes that it would transform life at Rome by inserting it halfway through the work he was engaged on at the time where it could be dramatised most strongly as an agent of disruption.[47] And although it is possible to see a new direction in Cicero's philosophy after Caesar's death, with a greater interest in ethical topics of relevance to the practical business of being a politician – glory, friendship, duty – it would be wrong to see an abrupt split, or to use the shift in emphasis as grounds for dividing what was written earlier as unrelated to the public sphere.

A neat indication of their unity comes in a letter to Atticus of 25 July 44, while Cicero was in southern Italy and hesitating whether to proceed on his journey to Greece. He had re-read the *Academica* while travelling and had noticed that he had unwittingly reused the preface to book 3 in *On glory*, which he had just sent to Atticus; he explains this by referring to a book of prefaces he has to hand when working.[48] This anecdote has interesting implications for Cicero's compositional practice, but it also underlines that works composed on either side of Caesar's death are, to at least some extent, part of the same project. Unfortunately this particular preface has not survived in either location, though its unwitting recycling would strongly suggest it was similar to what is found in other prefaces; and it is also worth noting the context of this letter. Cicero was, by then, excluded once again from political life, or rather had excluded himself; initial jubilation at Caesar's death had rapidly turned to disillusion. It is not clear that philosophy now served a very different purpose for him from the one it had served before Caesar's death.

The writing of philosophy, then, is presented as an alternative form of public activity, not as a retreat from it, even during Caesar's dictatorship. To this extent, these works are open to readings which allow for more to be at stake than simply the exposition of philosophical doctrine: it is possible for the reader to let their status as works by *Cicero* affect his or her approach. However, the ambition which Cicero manifests in his philosophy, with his claims both to make philosophy Latin and that the writing of philosophy is a suitable activity for an otiose politician, is in an uneasy counterpoint with a profound ambivalence about the future of Roman intellectual life.

Once again, the form of these works is significant. They embody a powerful ideal of intellectual community. But it is an ideal which is overwhelming placed in the past. Those dialogues which involve large and varied groups of people are all pre-civil war gatherings; when Cicero discusses philosophy in the present day, he does so, with the exception of Varro's appearance in the second edition of the *Academica*, only with Quintus and Atticus. Lively discussion between relatively disparate members of the elite is not, it is implied, a feature of the post-civil war world, and it is surely not coincidence that the books of *On ends* which are set in the very recent past feature those who will die in the coming conflict.[49] And it seems that, with the exception of Quintus, Atticus, and Cicero himself, all the characters who feature in *On ends 5*, *Hortensius*, the first edition of the *Academica*, and *On the nature of the gods*, which are all set before Cicero's exile, are also dead.[50]

In particular, it is curious that Brutus does not feature as an interlocutor in any of the philosophical treatises, though many are dedicated to him.[51] Possibly Brutus himself had made it clear that he did not appreciate being written into Cicero's dialogues after *Brutus*; perhaps Cicero felt constricted in portraying in a philosophical dialogue someone who had written independently on philosophical topics. But it is surely a choice worth noting; and one could argue that it reveals the narrowing of intellectual life which is underlined by the contrast in numbers of interlocutors between dialogues set before and after the civil war. Cicero's pedagogical ambitions are no longer exercised through face-to-face conversation with a younger generation but confined to written texts. The writing down of philosophical conversations has replaced holding them. And Brutus' presence in *Brutus* might reinforce this interpretation, since one of his most important functions is to embody the death of oratory, not least as a result of the deaths of his contemporaries. Brutus is denied the fruits of competitiveness which have been available to his predecessors.[52]

Yet, without wishing to stray too far into counter-factual speculation, the contemporary environment which Cicero depicts by implication in his philosophical treatises is arguably too gloomy. Cicero was not in either an intellectual or a social vacuum at this time. He had links of both kinds with certain Caesarians, declaiming with Hirtius and Pansa and sending his putative letter of advice to Balbus and Oppius for comment; and he was also engaged in literary debates with Caesar himself – who appeared to be more than happy to engage with Cicero on this territory. Balbus read the fifth book of *On ends* before its wider dissemination.[53] Had Cicero wished to create a philosophical coterie sited in the Rome of 46 and 45 it is hard to see that he would have been unable to do so; I suggest that this never occurred to him, or occurred only to be dismissed, precisely because he did feel that the political transformation had had profound reverberations in the intellectual sphere.

The *Philippics*

It remains to consider the *Philippics*, the set of fourteen speeches in which Cicero resisted the ambitions of Marcus Antonius and attempted to preserve a free republic. It is tempting to see these speeches as the glorious culmination of Cicero's public career, the point at which he emerges from his marginalisation during Caesar's dictatorship to take centre stage once more in a final, doomed attempt to preserve the Republic.

This is an excellent story. But it becomes more interesting once

140

the equivalence of the *Philippics* themselves to the free republic is inspected further. Cicero's oratory in the *Philippics* is complicit with profound changes that have already taken place in Roman political life and whose fixity he assumes. The nature of public debate and the penalties for failure have been transformed: and in accepting these changes, the *Philippics* end up transcribing not a glorious rebirth but what is, despite Cicero's hopes, an acknowledgement of failure even before the test of fighting.

The *Philippics* were, with one exception, delivered as speeches between September 43 and April 44, and Cicero seems to have disseminated texts of them rapidly.[54] We have already seen how they feature in his correspondence with *imperium*-holders during this period. Indeed, the circulation of these speeches and the relationship of spoken to written texts in this case itself demonstrates the transformation of public life. The Senate is now no longer the most important decision-making body: the key is rather the choices made by commanders in the field. It is not exactly that the Senate has lost all influence: but its effectiveness now depends on convincing military commanders of its effectiveness. In the winter of 44-43, maintaining the Senate's authority became enormously important precisely because the Senate had become so fragile in the face of the military power wielded by its *imperium*-holders, and the *Philippics* are a key part in keeping the performance at Rome going.

It is not coincidental, then, that the most famous and lengthy of the *Philippics*, the second, with its sustained attack on Marcus Antonius, was never delivered. More than that, there was no time at which it could have been delivered, and in this respect it differs from Cicero's other 'fictional' speeches, the *Verrines* and *On behalf of Milo*. These were all speeches which were connected with a particular trial, even though the circumstances which would have allowed for their delivery did not arise. But although the debate which Cicero presents the second *Philippic* as contributing to did take place, this speech was not delivered then; indeed, Cicero was not present in the Senate at that debate. One of the notable ironies of the whole situation is that Cicero, while gearing up to be the Senate's defender, did not attend the Senate between 2 September, when he delivered the first *Philippic*, and 20 December. He wrote the second *Philippic* in September and October, and it was finished by 25 October, when he sent a copy to Atticus for comment and to disseminate as he saw fit.[55] He made certain modifications in the light of Atticus' comments, and it seems likely that it was disseminated later in November, once Antonius had departed for his army in Gaul.

The immediate cause of Cicero's writing the second *Philippic* was Antonius' attack on him in the Senate on 19 September: it purports to be a response to that speech, delivered on that same day.[56] Antonius' speech, an attack on the whole of Cicero's career, was itself a response to the first *Philippic*, whose notable restraint of language and explicit disavowal of personal invective do not undermine its status as a thorough-going attack on Antonius' position within the Roman state.[57] That is, the train of events was initiated by Cicero's decision to become involved in the political situation at Rome by delivering that speech on 2 September, and presumably by a fairly rapid dissemination of what he had said. Antonius made it clear on 19 September that he looked to the contents of the first *Philippic* rather than its style, and regarded it as an attack on him; this in turn justified the tone Cicero adopted in the second *Philippic*.

However, although its most memorable passages may indeed be the vignettes of Antonius' debauchery – entering Curio's house through the roof-tiles (2.45), vomiting in the forum (2.63), or keeping a romantic assignation with his wife (2.77) – it is important to bear the structure of the speech in mind. It is bipartite, and the first part, (1-43) is a detailed refutation of the charges which Antonius had made against him. The first task of the second *Philippic* is to rescue Cicero's reputation from Antonius' attacks.[58] Nor, overall, does the speech advance the debate further than the position put forward in the first *Philippic*: an exhortation to Antonius to stop using the position he has taken over from Caesar as the basis for acting beyond the scope of his position as consul. Cicero is not yet leading a campaign of action against Antonius, but preparing the ground by attempting to win over the opinions of those in the Senate.

Both speeches are grounded in an appeal to a model of the Roman state in which the Senate's influence is heeded by its magistrates. It is the prospect of Antonius 'dismissing his bad advisers, giving up the Gallic provinces, and heeding the authority of the Senate' which encourages Cicero to give up his plans of travelling to Greece and return to Rome.[59] The ideal existence which Cicero ascribes to Antonius' grandfather, his namesake, that Marcus Antonius whose authority as an orator Cicero had appropriated in *On the orator*, is 'to be equal with others in freedom, but foremost in prestige'.[60] In the second speech, Cicero appeals to the suppression of the Catilinarian conspiracy as a model for senatorial action. There are references to his actions then in both the opening and closing paragraphs of the speech; and while it is important for Cicero to deploy this example given that the debate between him and Antonius now centres on personal authority and achievements, he also makes clear that he was acting at the Senate's behest: 'That consulship was mine in name, members of the Senate, but in reality it was yours: every decision, every official act, everything I did was done with the advice, authority and backing of this body.'[61] Antonius, on the other hand, has not only disregarded the Senate, but has terrorised them by the threat of armed force.[62]

It is essential for Cicero's argument to lay out the threat that Antonius poses to the state; and it is rhetorically effective for him to make clear that the stakes are now life and death.[63] That the penalty for being wrong is death is an indication of why Antonius must be resisted. And it is also effective for Cicero to draw attention to the paucity of senior figures. Early in the second *Philippic* he contrasts Antonius' disapproval of his consulship with the approval it met with at the time from those who had held the consulship, or were consuls-designate; and Cato is also listed.[64] There are interesting omissions from the list, and the impression that Cicero gives of the Senate's role in the suppression of the conspiracy is quite misleading.[65] But in addition to a rewriting of history which places Cicero at the heart of consensus there is also a profound sense of loss. He points out that the sixteen men who supported him are all dead, and only two of the consulars of 63 are still alive. These two, Lucius Cotta and Lucius Caesar, posed a potential problem for Cicero, since it does not seem that they supported him openly in 44: indeed, Caesar was Antonius' maternal uncle. But Cicero sidesteps the problem. Cotta serves Cicero's purpose well because he proposed the Thanksgiving in 63, though Cicero misplaces it in the chronology of events; and Caesar is useful, because he provides a contrast with the behaviour of his nephew, and enables Cicero to move back Antonius by means of the reflection that Antonius should have imitated his maternal uncle, but has not – choosing instead his stepfather, one of the conspirators who was executed in 63.

Nonetheless, one could argue that the melancholy created by this passage is somewhat misleading. It is impossible without accurate knowledge of life-expectancies to determine how many consulars at a certain date one would expect still to be alive twenty years later: but a high death-rate is not surprising, given that the youngest in the sample would be into their forties at the time of holding the consul-ship. And the only figures on the list known to have died other than of natural causes are Crassus, who was killed in Parthia in 53, and Pompeius and Cato during the civil war. This is not a list of internecine attrition. One could certainly be drawn up, and would include a number of the consuls of the period between 63 and the civil war; and Cicero is here economically drawing on the sense of a Senate bereft of wisdom and tradition while in fact using a list of older names – whose absence also indicates Cicero's seniority. There are only two men surviving whose experience of public affairs goes back further, at the highest level, than his.

The later *Philippics* work within a rather different set of con-straints. They are the record of actual contributions to senatorial debates (or, in the case of the fourth and sixth, summaries of those contributions to a public meeting immediately afterwards) and seem to be primarily concerned with getting the decision that Cicero wants. Nor is he always successful. His resistance to sending an embassy to Antonius at the beginning of January 43, recorded in the fifth *Philippic*, was unsuccessful; the sixth speech, to the people, attempts to gloss over this failure. He did not manage to get the situation described as a 'war';[66] and his proposal, in the tenth *Philippic*, concerning the situation in the east in the aftermath of the murder of Trebonius, fell. The twelfth speech shows that Cicero did at one point consider participating himself in an embassy to An-tonius. Yet all these setbacks are recorded in written form.

The *Philippics* do something which we do not find elsewhere in Cicero's oratorical corpus: they provide a narrative of unfolding events as they develop over a period of months. Moreover, the narrative does not just concern facts. It is important too to record the stages of decision-making. Hence the inclusion into the set of speeches of the fourth, to the people, which summarises what the reader may already know from the third. So it would seem that the people's favourable response to Cicero's proposal is also an important part of the story he is attempting to tell.

It would be possible to interpret this extended narrative as the product of genuinely changed political circumstances. Cicero is producing speeches in which the outcome of a debate is the most important thing because he is engaged in a struggle over a period of months to affect the course of events. The *Philippics* are not, then, novel for the sake of innovation but because Cicero faced what was, for him, a new challenge: an internal domestic crisis which persisted over a period of months.[67] For the first time in twenty years, Cicero had a serious opportunity to influence events.

The difficulty with this interpretation is not that Cicero did not play a leading part in events, or that they were not of the gravity with which he invested them. And it would be a mistake to underestimate what was at stake in the crisis, or to divorce the texts that we have from the events which generated them. But we should beware too simplistic a relationship between the two.

For all their apparently straightforward recording of events, the *Philippics* are also carefully considered texts. When Cicero gave them the name '*Philippics*' he was not simply joking with Brutus.[68] In evoking the comparison, he attempted two things: to underscore the nature of the threat from Antonius through the analogy with Philip's attack on Athens' freedom; and to reiterate the comparison between himself and Demosthenes, a resonant move with Cicero back to the time of his consular orations, if not before. That is, the *Philippics*' being the record of crucial political debates is not incompatible with their also being self-conscious artefacts. Indeed, the novelty of 44-43 is not just that Cicero is once more directing the state; it is that the struggle is textual. I would suggest, in fact, that Cicero's juniors have been highly attentive pupils. The reticence in producing texts which we have observed among the leading orators in the generations before him has gone, and it is enormously compelling to see Cicero as one of the motives for change. He and Caesar, in radically different ways, demonstrated to other politicians how to transcend the limitations of memoir and produce texts which enact contemporaneous engagement with public life.[69]

The *Philippics* are records of an unfolding struggle and also weapons in that struggle: not simply because they communicate with a wider audience than initially heard Cicero but because they memorialise Cicero engaging in a particular set of public actions. It is in their demonstration of Cicero's capacities as a public figure as much as in what they say that their effectiveness lies. They can be seen as the ultimate stage in Cicero's creation of himself as a public figure through writing himself as a public figure.

It would be wrong to end this study, then, with an unrelieved picture of failure: Cicero's ultimate failure as a public figure is accompanied by a demonstration of the success with which he had transformed the potential of writing as a means of being a public figure. I have attempted to chart the transformation of writing among the elite in the half century or so between Cicero's first works and his death, and repeatedly Cicero is at the forefront of developing ways of writing which open up new possibilities for the public figure.

Naturally there are also dangers in this focus on Cicero: he was not operating in an intellectual wasteland and his achievements as a writer gain much of their meaning from the interaction with other writings that they spring from.[70] This was an intellectual age, though the loss of so much of its writing makes reconstructions speculative. But it does seem that much that was done was highly scholarly – and of course much too was written in Greek. Cicero's achievement remains distinct: he took intellectual activity and inserted it into the public arena. We need to reunite public career and writing when reading Cicero not simply because the one can illuminate the other, nor even just because writing helped Cicero gain his ends as a politician, important as both these approaches are. Cicero's writing finally compels our attention because he made being an intellectual and a writer into part of what it meant to be a public figure.

Notes

Introduction

1. Sen. *Ep.* 108.30.
2. Accounts of Cicero's life can be found in Rawson (1983); Stockton (1971); Mitchell (1979, 1991).
3. 'Elite' is too convenient a term to abandon, despite its inevitable imprecision. I understand by it any Roman citizen whose wealth matched the census criterion for the equestrian order, including members of the Senate. By using it I do not intend to elide the enormous differences in wealth, status and activity which existed within this group.
4. Cic. *Clu.* 141, *de Or.* 2.223-5.
5. Rawson (1985: 146 [Antonius], 227-8 [autobiography]).
6. cf. Kenney (1982); Starr (1987).
7. cf. Gruen (1992); Gowers (1993) 50-76; Habinek and Schiesaro (1997); Laurence and Berry (1998); Krostenko (2001). It is of course true that Cicero's earliest work, *On Invention*, is likely to have entered the public domain before, and probably substantially before, he pled his first case. But as I shall argue in Chapter 1, one of the many striking features of *On Invention* is its confidence in discussing public affairs despite the obscurity of its author.
8. Hellegouarc'h (1963) 295-320; Goodwin (2001).
9. Plin. *H.N.* 7.117.
10. Cf. in particular Stroh (1975); Classen (1985); May (1988); Craig (1993); Vasaly (1993); May (2002).
11. Douglas (1968), 1.

1. Genre

1. *Brut.* 61-2. On *laudationes funebres*, see Flower (1996) 145-50.
2. Humbert (1925); Stroh (1975) 31-45; cf. Riggsby (1995).
3. *Or.* 132; 'They say that M. Antonius, a brilliant man, was accustomed to say that he had never written down a speech precisely in order that he could deny that he had said something if it was ever unhelpful for him to

have said it' (*Clu.* 140: 'hominem ingeniosum, M. Antonium, aiunt solitum esse dicere "idcirco se nullam umquam orationem scripsisse ut, si quid aliquando non opus eset ab se esse dictum, posset negare dixisse" ').

4. Crawford (1984) 7-21; Crawford (2002).

5. It is also worth asking whether the gender of the defendants played any part in his decision not to write up.

6. Axer (1979).

7. Kinsey (1971) 5-6. The precise dating of *On behalf of Varenus* is uncertain, but its date is generally agreed to be before 70 BC (Crawford 1994, 7-9).

8. *Inst.* 4.1.74, 4.2.26; 5.10.69, 5.13.28; 6.1.49; 7.1.9, 12; 7.2.10, 22, 36; 8.3.22; 9.2.56. See Crawford (1994) 11-15 for other ancient testimonia.

9. Alexander (1990): *repetundae*, nos. 131, 135, 139, 140, 144, 158, 170, 172, 174; Cluentius affair, 147, 148, 149; Vestal Virgins, 167-9. Cicero was involved tangentially with the Cluentius affair, as he defended Scamander, unsuccessfully.

10. Fonteius, whom Cicero defended on *repetundae* charges.

11. Hortensius' first case was in 95 BC; and between the resumption of judicial activity after Sulla's dictatorship and his consulship his involvement in nine trials is attested. Between his consulship and Cicero's, only one case is known (a defence of L. Vargunteius on bribery charges); its dating is very uncertain and may predate his consulship.

12. Gotoff (1993) xxxii-xl; Bringmann (1986).

13. Hall (2002) 281-3.

14. *Phil.* 3.8; 3.15; 3.25.

15. *Phil.* 2.7-9.

16. Plut. *Cic.* 41.6 implies the existence of a written text.

17. Butler (2002).

18. Tac. *Dial.* 21.6.

19. Courtney (1993) 152.

20. Lightfoot (1999) 68; Aeschylus' play and the surviving fragments are discussed in Krumeich, Pechstein and Seidensticker (1999) 125-30.

21. See Courteney (1993) 149-78. On *de temporibus suis*, see Harrison (1990).

22. *Leg.* 1.1-5; *Div.* 1.106.

23. Rawson (1971) 75-88.

24. Courtney (1993) 118.

25. Steel (2001) 46-7.

26. Goldberg (1995) 135-6.

27. Rawson (1985) 227-8.

28. Courtney (1993) 156-73.

29. *Cons.* fr. 10.

30. *Cons.* fr. 6, 7.

31. *Cons.* fr. 8, 12.

32. *Cons.* fr. 11.

33. *Att.* 2.4.3; 2.6.1; 2.7.1.
34. Goar (1987).
35. Cf. Corbeill (2002).
36. *de Or.* 1.5.
37. There is a wide range of opinions about the dating: e.g. Rawson (1985) 19, 'Some time in the 80s'; Kennedy (1994) 117, 'Sometime between 92 and 88'; Corbeill (2002) 28, 'composed in the late 90s'; see Corbeill (2002), 31-4.
38. *Phil.* 2.27; *Div.* 1.72.
39. *Brut.* 306.
40. *Brut.* 306-10; for Philo, see Brittain (2001) 64-6.
41. Rawson (1985) 149; cf. Quint. *Inst.* 3.1.19-20.
42. Corbeill (2002) 32.
43. *Inv.* 2.9-10.
44. Suetonius *de grammaticis et rhetoribus* 26.1.
45. Rawson (1985) 222.
46. Wiseman (1998).
47. Rawson (1985) 284.
48. *Leg.* 1.5-11.
49. Görler (1988); Sharples (1986); Zetzel (1995) 13-29.
50. See Cugusi (1983) 160-1; Shackleton Bailey (1988); Beard (2002); White (2003).
51. Shackleton Bailey (1965) 59-76.
52. Nepos *Life of Atticus* 16.3: 'ei rei sunt indicio praeter eos libros, in quibus de eo facit mentionem, qui in uulgus sunt editi, XI uolumina epistularum, ab consulatu eius usque ad extremum tempus ad Atticum missarum: quae qui legat, non multum desideret historiam contextam eorum temporum.'
53. *Att.* 16.5.
54. *Fam.* 16.17.1 (to Tiro) may also support the idea of a collection, though it may refer only to Tiro's desire to have his letters preserved with Cicero's records.
55. *Phil.* 2.7: 'at etiam litteras, quas me sibi misisse diceret, recitauit homo et humanitatis expers et uitae communis ignarus. quis enim umquam, qui paulum modo bonorum consuetudinem nosset, litteras ad se ab amico missas offensione aliqua interposita in medium protulit palamque recitauit? quid est aliud tollere ex uita uitae societatem, tellere amicorum conloquia absentium? quam multa ioca solent esse in epistulis, quae prolata si sint, inepta uideantur, quam multa seria, neque tamen ullo modo diuolganda!'
56. Cugusi (1983) 44-5; Nicholson (1994).
57. Cugusi (1970) gathers together the evidence: see vol. 1, pp. 124-9 for Verres' letters.
58. *Brut.* 211.
59. But cf. Hutchinson (1998).
60. See now Craig (2002) 515-31.

61. The sole exception is *Fam.* 7.27.

2. Cicero as a Public Figure

1. Cicero's forensic self-presentation is handled exhaustively by May (1988).

2. For accounts of the events of 63, see *CAH* 9^2 338-67; Crawford (1978) 155-70.

3. *Att.* 2.1.3.

4. It seems likely, in fact, that he never disseminated a written version of his defence of Gaius Piso. Both the other defences had clear political ramifications.

5. Only more senior magistrates had the right to summon assemblies of the people (Lintott (1999) 43-9), and opportunities for lengthy speech-making in the Senate were normally confined to this group too. *On the Command of Gnaeus Pompeius*, given in 66 when Cicero was praetor, was his first significant piece of deliberative oratory.

6. Stroh (1975) 51-4.

7. *Att.* 1.19.10.

8. *Att.* 1.20.6.

9. *Att.* 2.1.1-2.

10. cf. McDermott (1972).

11. *Sull.* 2: 'quo quidem genere non uterer orationis, iudices, hoc tempore, si mea solum interesset: multis enim mihi locis et data facultas est et saepe dabitur de mea laude dicendi.'

12. On *regnum* see Berry (1996) 174-8.

13. Quint. *Inst.* 9.3.40 ('uestrum iam hic factum deprehenditur, patres conscripti, non meum, ac pulcherrimum quidem factum, uerum, ut dixi, non meum, sed uestrum'); 9.3.45 ('uos enim statuistis, uos sententiam dixistis, uos iudicastis'). Cf. Crawford (1994) 215-22.

14. *Sull.* 67 with Berry (1996) ad loc.

15. cf. Drummond (1995) 108-15.

16. *Att.* 1.16.6.

17. *Att.* 1.17.8-9.

18. Clodius also called Cicero a *rex*, king (*Att.*1.16.10). Stockton (1971) 143-75; Mitchell (1991) 83-8.

19. *Att.* 1.16.15.

20. *Att.* 2.3.4.

21. 'haec mihi cum in eo libro in quo multa sunt scripta ἀριστοκρατικῶς Calliope ipsa praescripserit ....'

22. Courtney (1993) 156-73.

23. cf. *Arch.* 12-14.

24. Catul. 64.321; Lucr. 1.731.

25. *iam* in l.10 suggests that clear sight has only recently become possible – with Cicero's translation of Aratus?

26. Courtney (1993) 159, 172. An alternative reading is 'O fortunatam natam *te* consule Romam'; see Goldberg (1995) 167 n.17.

27. *Pis.* 6.

28. cf. *Flac.* 102: 'Nones of December, what a day in my year of consulship you were! A day which I can truly call the birthday of this city, or certainly the day of salvation' ('O Nonae illae Decembres quae me consule fuistis! quem ego diem uere natalem huius urbis aut certe salutarem appellare possum').

29. *Fam.* 5.7.

30. *Fam.* 5.7.3.

31. Meier (1962); Gruen (1971) 83-5; Seager (1979) 68-71.

32. *Arch.* 26.

33. Strabo 11.1.6.

34. Note in particular *Catil.* 1.6-10 (Cicero emphasises the extent of his knowledge); *Catil.* 1.27-9 (the state addresses him); *Catil.* 4.1-5 (Cicero will face anything if he can preserve the state); *Catil.* 4.23-4 (reassurance to the Senate that they have a consul who will protect them).

35. *Catil.* 1.30: '... non nulli sunt in hoc ordine qui aut ea quae imminent non uideant aut ea quae uident dissimulent: qui spem Catilinae mollibus sententiis conroborauerunt; quorum auctoritate multi non solum improbi uerum etiam imperiti, si in hunc animaduertissem, crudeliter et regie factum esse dicerent.'

36. Tatum (1999).

37. Dio 39.20.

38. *Har.* 11: 'quam primum inimicus ipse in illa tempestate ac nocte rei publicae, cum cetera scelera stilo illo impuro Sex. Cloeli ore tincto conscripsisset, ne una quidem attigit littera religionis; deinde eandem domum populus Romanus, cuius est summa potestas omnium rerum, comitiis centuriatis omnium aetatum ordinumque suffragiis eodem iure esse iussit quo fuisset; postea uos, patres conscripti, non quo dubia res esset, sed ut huic furiae, si diutius in hac urbe quam delere cuperet maneret, uox interdiceretur, decreuistis ut de mearum aedium religione ad pontificum conlegium referretur.'

39. *Har.* 2: 'an potest grauioribus a me uerbis uulnerari quam est statim in facto ipso a grauissimo uiro, P. Seruilio, confectus ac trucidatus? cuius si iam uim et grauitatem illam singularem ac paene diuinam adsequi possem tamen non dubito quin ea tela quae coniecerit inimicus quam ea quae conlega patris emisit leuiora atque hebetiora esse uideantur.'

40. Lenaghan (1969) 55-6. Clodius' mother and Servilius were first cousins.

41. *Har.* 60-1: 'fuit quondam ita firma haec ciuitas et ualens ut neglegentiam senatus uel etiam iniurias ciuium ferre posset. iam non potest. aerarium nullum est, uectigalibus non fruuntur qui redemerunt, auctoritas principum cecidit, consensus ordinum est diuulsus, iudicia perierunt, suffragia descripta tenentur a paucis, bonorum animus ad nutum nostri ordinis expeditus iam non erit, ciuem qui se pro patriae salute opponat inuidiae frustra posthac requiretis. qua re hunc statum qui nunc est qualiscumque est, nulla alia re nisi concordia retinere possumus; ....'

42. *Har.* 61: 'atque ego hanc orationem, patres conscripti, tam tristem, tam grauem non suscepissem, non quin hanc personam et has partis, honoribus populi Romani, uestris plurimis ornamentis mihi tributis, deberem et possem sustinere, sed tamen facile tacentibus ceteris reticuissem; sed haec oratio omnis fuit non auctoritatis meae, sed publicae religionis.'

43. *Har.* 18: '... neque is sum qui, si cui forte uideor plus quam ceteri qui aeque atque ego sunt occupati uersari in studio litterarum, his delecter aut utar omnino litteris quae nostros animos deterrent atque auocant a religione.'

44. *Har.* 19: 'deinde, si quid habui oti, etiam cognoui multa homines doctos sapientisque et dixisse et scripta de deorum immortalium numine reliquisse; quae quamquam diuinitus perscripta uideo, tamen eius modi sunt ut ea maiores nostri docuisse illos, non ab illis didicisse uideantur.'

45. See *de Or.* 2.154, *Rep.* 2.28-30, *Tusc.* 4.2-3 where Cicero demolishes this view directly. See further Rawson (1985) 282-316; Gruen (1990) 158-70.

46. Sall. [*Cic.*] 6: 'egeris, oro te, Cicero, prefeceris quidlibet: satis est perpessos esse: etiamne aures nostras odio tuo onerabis, etiamne molestissimis uerbis insectabere?'

47. Sen. *Con.* 3 pr. 8 ('His eloquence deserted Cicero in his poetry'; Cassius Severus is the speaker); Quint. *Inst.* 11.1.24; Tac. *Dial.* 21.6; Juv. 10.122-6.

48. Cicero quotes the line 'Let arms yield ...' when considering his achievement as consul in *On Duties* (*Off.* 1.77); but though this passage is further testimony to the continuing criticism of the line it is of limited relevance to the debates of the 50s.

49. On *On the Orator* see May and Wisse (2001); Leeman, Pinkster et al. (1981-); *Rhetorica* 6 (special issue devoted to *On the Orator*); Wisse (1989); Hall (1994).

50. *de Or.* 1.211: 'sin autem quaereremus quis esset is, qui ad rem publicam moderandam usum et scientiam et studium suum contulisset, definerem hoc modo: qui quibus rebus utilitas rei publicae pareretur augereturque, teneret eisque uteretur, hunc rei publicae rectorem et consili publici auctorem esse habendum, ...'

51. *Phil.* 8.14; V. Max. 5.3.2.

52. *de Or.* 1.213-15.

53. *de Or.* 1.38.

54. At 2.39-40 Cicero has Antonius admit that he took a contrary position during the first day's discussion simply for the sake of argument. Cf. Vickers (1988) 32-4.

55. *Q.Fr.* 3.5.1: 'de optimo statu ciuitatis et de optimo ciue.' On the

work's composition, see Schmidt (2001) and the summary, with bibliography, in Zetzel (1995) 3-4.

56. Powell (1994).

57. 'beata ciuium uita ... ut opibus firma, copiis locuples, gloria ampla, uirtute honesta sit' (preserved in Cic. *Att.* 8.11.1).

58. cf. Powell (1990) 119-33.

59. *Rep.* 6.13: 'nihil est enim illi principi deo qui omnem mundum regit, quod quidem in terris fiat, acceptius quam concilia coetusque hominum iure sociati, quae ciuitates appellantur; harum rectores et conseruatores hinc profecti huc reuertuntur.'

60. *Rep.* 29: 'hanc tu exerce in optimis rebus! sunt autem optimae curae de salute patriae, quibus agitatus et exercitatus animus uelocius in hanc sedem et domum suam peruolabit; ....'

61. *de Or.* 1-2: 'cogitanti mihi saepe numero et memoria uetera repetenti perbeati fuisse, Quinte frater, illi uideri solent, qui in optima re publica, cum et honoribus et rerum gestarum gloria florerent, eum uitae cursum tenere potuerunt, ut uel in negotio sine periculo uel in otio cum dignitate esse possent; ac fuit cum mihi quoque initium requiescendi atque animum ad utriusque nostrum praeclara studia referendi fore iustum et prope ab omnibus concessum arbitrarer, si infinitus forensium rerum labor et ambitionis occupatio decursu honorum, etiam aetatis flexu constitisset. quam spem cogitationum et consiliorum meorum cum graues communium temporum tum uarii nostri casus fefellerunt; ....'

62. *Leg.* 1.8.

63. *Leg.* 1.9: 'historia uero nec institui potest nisi praeparato otio, nec exiguo tempore absolui ....'

64. *Rep.* 1.1-3.

65. *Rep.* 1.1.2: 'M. uero Catoni homini ignoto et nouo, quo omnes qui isdem rebus studemus quasi exemplari ad industriam uirtutemque ducimur, certe licuit Tusculi se in otio delectare ....'

3. Ciceronian Communities

1. Gelzer (1969) Brunt (1988) 351-81; Spielvogel (1993) 5-19.

2. Beard and Crawford (1999) 60-71 provide a concise introduction to the debate.

3. *de Or.* 3.228-30; *Brut.* 229ff.

4. *Quinct.* 1: 'quae res in ciuitate duae plurimum possunt, eae contra nos ambae faciunt in hoc tempore, summa gratia et eloquentia; quarum alteram, C. Aquili, uereor, alteram metuo. eloquentia Q. Hortensi ne me in dicendo impediat, non nihil commoueor, gratia Sex. Naeui ne P. Quinctio noceat, id uero non mediocriter pertimesco.'

5. Kinsey (1971) 51-3.

6. 'I make some allowance for your anger, I give some leeway to your youth, I make some concessions for our friendship, and I give some weight

to your father' (*Sul.* 46: 'permitto aliquid iracundiae tuae, do adulescentiae, cedo amicitiae, tribuo parenti'); 'I shall deal fairly gently with you, Atratinus, because your modesty restrains my speech, and I ought to have regard for the obligations which link me to you and your father' (*Cael.* 7: 'tecum, Atratine, agam lenius, quod et pudor tuus moderatur orationi meae et meum erga te parentemque tuum beneficium tueri debeo').

7. 'I never thought, gentlemen of the jury, that Decimus Laelius, the son of an excellent man and himself enjoying solid expectations of high office, should take up this prosecution …' (*Flac.* 2: 'numquam tamen existimaui, iudices, D. Laelium, optimi uiri filium, optima ipsum spe praeditum summae dignitatis, eam suscepturum accusationem …').

8. *Rab. Post.* 7.

9. Steel (2001) 58-66.

10. *Balb.* 1: 'si auctoritates patronorum in iudiciis ualent, ab amplissimis uiris L. Corneli causa defensa est; si usus, a peritissimis; si ingenia, ab eloquentissimis; si studia, ab amicissimis et cum beneficiis cum L. Cornelio tum maxima familiaritate coniunctis.'

11. Steel (2001) 108-10.

12. Shackleton Bailey (1971) 179-85.

13. cf. e.g. *Att.* 1.14 and *Att.* 1.16 with *Q.Fr.* 2.1.

14. *Att.* 1.5.2. Nepos records that Atticus never quarrelled with his sister (*Att.* 17.1).

15. Nepos, *Att.* 1, 2, 16 on friendships, esp. with Hortensius.

16. Cicero's letters to Caelius from this period are *Fam.* 2.8-15; Caelius', *Fam.* 8.1-14. See Schneider (1998) 448-606.

17. *Fam.* 8.1.1: 'quod tibi discedens pollicitus sum me omnis res urbanas diligentissime tibi perscripturum, data opera paraui qui sic omnia perse-queretur ut uerear ne tibi nimium arguta haec sedulitas uideatur; tametsi tu scio quam sis curiosus et quam omnibus peregrinantibus gratum sit mini-marum quoque rerum quae domi gerantur fieri certiores.'

18. *Fam.* 2.8.1: 'quid? tu me hoc tibi mandasse existimas, ut mihi gladiatorum compositiones, ut uadimonia dilata et Chresti compilationem mitteres et ea quae nobis, cum Romae sumus, narrare nemo audeat?' Cf. *Q.Fr.* 1.1.1.

19. *Fam.* 2.8.1: 'scribent alii, multi nuntiabunt, perferet multa etiam ipse rumor.'

20. cf. *Fam.* 12.22.1.

21. Cicero published his part in the (successful) defence, as *On behalf of Caelius*.

22. Caelius was hoping for Cicero's assistance in putting on a fine wild beast display during his aedileship (*Fam.* 8.9.3; 8.8.10; 8.6.5).

23. e.g. *Fam.* 2.8.2.

24. cf. Steel (2001) 1-2.

25. They are collected in book 13 of the *Fam.* collection. Cf. Cotton (1986).

26. On one occasion (*Fam.* 13.6) the letter refers to an earlier conversation between Cicero and the addressee about the men he is recommending.

27. *Fam.* 13.31: 'C. Flauio, honesto et ornato equite Romano, utor ualde familiariter; fuit enim generi mei, C. Pisonis, pernecessarius meque diligentissime obseruant et ipse et L. Clauius, frater eius. quapropter uelim honoris mei causa, quibus rebus honeste et pro tua dignitate poteris, quam honorificentissime et quam liberalissime C. Flauium tractes; id mihi sic erit gratum ut gratius esse nihil possit. sed praeterea tibi adfirmo (neque id ambitione adductus facio sed cum familiaritate et necessitudine tum etiam ueritate) te ex C. Flaui officio et obseruantia et praeterea splendore atque inter suos gratia magnam uoluptatem esse capturum. uale.'

28. *Fam.* 13.29.1; 13.43.1; 13.50.2; 13.77.3.

29. *Fam.* 13.10.4; 13.20; 13.28a.2; 13.38; 13.45; 13.46.

30. *Fam.* 13.6.

31. *Att.* 2.20.3.

32. *Fam.* 13.6.3: 'mirificum genus commendationis.'

33. Cicero makes no reference to having met L. Iulius, and if, as the letter implies, Iulius was then in Africa, he may never have done. The apparent lack of any personal connection between Cicero and Iulius surely works against the identification proposed by Shackleton Bailey of this Iulius with a friend of Atticus (Shackleton Bailey (1965) 355).

34. *Fam.* 13.6.4: 'harum litterarum uis quanta fuerit propediem iudicabo tibique, ut confido, gratias agam.'

35. *Fam.* 13.15, and cf. Shackleton Bailey (1977) ad loc.

36. *Fam.* 13.15.3: 'genere nouo sum litterarum ad te usus ut intellegeres non uulgarem esse commendationem.'

37. Though in the case of *Fam.* 13.15 it is at least worth asking whether Precilius even existed.

38. *Fam.* 4.7-11, 4.13-15, 5.21, 6.1-8, 6.10-14, 6.20-2.

39. Which is not to conceal the differences generated by the differences between correspondents, both in standing and in connection to Cicero.

40. *Fam.* 6.20.1: 'dederam triduo ante pueris Cn. Planci litteras ad te; eo nunc ero breuior teque, ut antea consolabar, hoc tempore monebo.' The earlier letter does not survive. Cf. *Fam.* 4.8.1.

41. *Fam.* 5.21.4.

42. *Fam.* 4.9.2.

43. *Fam.* 5.21.5.

44. *Fam.* 6.1.1.

45. *Fam.* 6.10b.1; 6.22.

46. *Fam.* 6.3.1.

47. *Fam.* 4.14.

48. *Fam.* 4.8.1.

49. *Fam.* 4.13.6; 6.5.4; 6.10a.1; 6.6.13.

50. *Fam.* 4.14.2; 6.6.4; 6.21.1 (shared with correspondent).

51. *Fam.* 6.6.5-8.

52. *Fam.* 6.6.1.

53. *Fam.* 4.13.6; 6.10a.2; 6.12.2.

54. Caesar's mercy: *Fam.* 4.13.5; 6.6.8; 6.10b.2; 6.13.2; likely outcome of a Pompeian victory, 4.9.2; 4.14.1; 6.4.1; 6.21.1.

55. These letters were sent only shortly before the meeting of the Senate at which Caesar agreed that Marcellus could return to Rome (and at which Cicero delivered his *On behalf of Marcellus*) and it is likely that they are linked to the efforts of his friends to have him recalled.

56. 'etsi eo te adhuc consilio usum intellego ut id reprehendere non audeam, non quin ab eo ipse dissentiam sed quod ea te sapientia esse iudicem ut meum consilium non anteponam tuo, tamen et amicitiae nostrae uetustas et tua summa erga me beneuolentia, quae mihi iam a pueritia tua cognita est, me hortata est ut ea scriberem ad te quae et saluti tuae conducere arbitrarer et non aliena esse ducerem a dignitate.'

57. *Fam.* 4.8.2.

58. *Fam.* 4.7.2.

59. *Fam.* 4.7.3.

60. *Fam.* 4.7.4: '... tamen id cogitare deberes, ubicumque esses, te fore in eius ipsius quem fugeres potestate.' Cf. 4.8.2.

61. *Fam.* 4.8.2.

62. *Fam.* 4.7.3 (Caesar is reluctant because he is not sure of Marcellus' gratitude).

63. The only other speech with a large audience was *On behalf of Ligarius*.

64. *Fam.* 7.1, 7.2.

65. *Fam.* 7.3.1: 'sollicitum autem te habebat cogitatio cum offici tum etiam periculi mei: si manerem in Italia, uerebare ne officio deessem; si proficiscerer ad bellum, periculum te meum commouebat.'

66. *Fam.* 7.3.3: 'si te uictori nolles aut non auderes committere.'

67. *Fam.* 7.3.6: 'haec tecum coram malueram; sed quia longius fiebat, uolui per litteras eadem, ut haberes quid diceres si quando in uituperatores meos incidisses. sunt enim qui, cum meus interitus nihil fuerit rei publicae profuturus, criminis loco putent esse quod uiuam; quibus ego certo scio non uideri satis multos perisse.'

68. *Fam.* 10.1.2, 10.27.2; 10.28.3; 11.25.1; 12.7.1; 12.8.1; 12.9.1; 12.23.2; 12.28.3; *ad Brut.* 2.1.3.

69. To Decimus Brutus (*Fam.* 11.5.1-2): 'qua re hortatione tu quidem non eges, si ne in illa quidem re quae a te gesta est post hominum memoriam maxima hortatorem desiderasi; illud tamen breuiter significandum uidetur, populum Romanum omnia se exspectare atque in te aliquando reciperandae libertatis omnem spem ponere.'

70. To Plancus (*Fam.* 10.3.3): 'incumbe, per deos immortalis, in eam curam et cogitationem quae tibi summam dignitatem et gloriam adferat; unus autem est, hoc praesertim tempore, per tot annos re publica diuexata, rei publicae bene gerendae cursus ad gloriam.'

71. *Fam.* 12.2.1.
72. *Fam.* 11.6a.2.
73. *Fam.* 12.24.2.
74. *ad Brut.* 2.4.2.
75. *Fam.* 10.6.1.
76. *Fam.* 12.25.1.
77. *ad Brut.* 2.5.1.
78. *Fam.* 10.12.2-3.
79. *ad Brut.* 2.2.1.
80. *ad Brut.* 2.3.4.
81. *Fam.* 10.33.5.
82. *ad Brut.* 1.5.2.
83. See Griffin (1997).
84. *Fam.* 9.8.
85. *Fam.* 9.8.1: 'quin coniunctionem studiorum amorisque nostri quo possem litterarum genere declararem.'
86. *Fam.* 9.8.1: 'puto fore ut, cum legeris, mirere nos id locutos esse inter nos quod numquam locuti sumus, sed nosti morem dialogorum.'
87. Cicero's dialogues, unlike some of Plato's, do not pose insoluble dating conundrums.
88. The preface to Cicero's version of Plato's *Timaeus* refers to a conversation between him, Nigidius Figulus, and Cratippus, at Ephesus in 51 BC. But the body of the work itself does not seem to have been a dialogue.
89. *de Or.* 1.30.
90. *Rep.* 1.32.
91. *de Or.* 1.24-6.
92. *de Or.* 2.1-2.
93. Zetzel (1972) 177-8.
94. *Sen.* 1-2.
95. *Sen.* 3: 'omnem autem sermonem tribuimus ... Marco Catoni seni, quo maiorum auctoritatem haberet oratio; apud quem Laelium et Scipionem facimus admirantes quod is tam facile senectutem ferat, eisque eum respondentem. qui si eruditius uidebitur disputare, quam consueuit ipse in suis libris, attribuito litteris Graecis, quarum constat eum perstudiosum fuisse in senectute.'
96. Nonetheless, the meeting *could* have happened – Laelius and Scipio were in Rome at the date of the dialogue.

4. Failure

1. Asc. *Mil.* 42; Dio 40.54; Plut. *Cic.* 35.
2. Settle (1963); Stone (1980); Crawford (1984) 210-18; Marshall (1987).
3. Asconius' testimony gives no evidence as to when the first version began to be circulated. But if it was derived from the trial – that is, if we

reject the possibility that it was a much later forgery, even an unwitting one such as a rhetorical exercise – then there seems no reason to posit a delay. Of course, it is unlikely that the version circulated very widely, but as even a narrow circulation is likely to have included those whose opinion Cicero valued it is easy to see why it might have become a factor in his decision to write his own version.

4. cf. Berry (2000) 169.

5. Calvus had recently initiated the Atticist/ Asianist controversy with his new spare style of speaking; Calvus himself might well have been dead by the time of Milo's trial, but the controversy had sufficient vitality to keep it alive through the civil war period, at least until Cicero responded to what he perceived as its attack on his own oratory in *Brutus* and *Orator*. Cicero had himself been compelled by Pompeius into a range of uncongenial forensic activity in the late 50s, the low point of which was his humiliating and unsuccessful defence of his former enemy Gabinius on extortion charges in the autumn of 54.

6. *Fam.* 7.2.2-3.

7. *Att.* 3.12.2.

8. But we are in a hall of mirrors. It is perfectly possible that *Mil.* 1 is the first reference to Cicero's fear in relation to this case, and that subsequent ancient commentators on the case have interpreted what was simply a rhetorical gesture to draw attention to Pompeius' show of force as a genuine description of Cicero's state of mind at the trial.

9. *Mil.* 30: 'qui hoc fato natus est, ut ne se quidem seruare potuerit quin una rem publicam uosque seruaret.'

10. *Mil.* 83.

11. *Mil.* 8, 83. The five are Servilius Ahala, who, according to tradition, killed Spurius Maelius in 439 BC when the latter resisted the dictator Cincinnatus; Scipio Nasica, who led the attack on Tiberius Gracchus in 133 BC and was subsequently sent on an embassy to Asia Minor, where he died; L. Opimius, who as consul in 121 BC put down the disturbances connected with Gaius Gracchus and, although acquitted at his first trial was subsequently convicted on charges arising from the Jugurthine war; C. Marius, who followed up his part in the deaths of Apuleius and his followers in 100 BC with an extended trip to Asia Minor; and Cicero himself, whose suppression of the Catilinarian conspiracy led to directly to his exile.

12. *Mil.* 5: 'quid enim nobis duobus, iudices, laboriosius, quid magis sollicitum, magis exercitum dici aut fingi potest, qui spe amplissimorum praemiorum ad rem publicam adducti metu crudelissimorum suppliciorum carere non possumus? equidem ceteras tempestates et procellas in illis dumtaxat fluctibus contionum semper putaui Miloni esse subeundas, quia semper pro bonis contra improbos senserat, in iudicio uero et in eo consilio, in quo ex cunctis ordinibus amplissimi uiri iudicarent, numquam existimaui spem ullam esse habituros Milonis inimicos ad eius non modo salutem exstinguendam, sed etiam gloriam per talis uiros infringendam.'

158

13. *Mil.* 96-7: 'addit haec, quae certe uera sunt, fortis et sapientis uiros non tam praemia sequi solere recte factorum quam ipsa recte facta; se nihil in uita nisi praeclarissime fecisse, si quidem nihil sit praestabilius uiro quam periculis patriam liberare. beatos esse, quibus ea res honori fuerit a suis civibus, nec tamen eos miseros, qui beneficio ciuis suos uicerint. sed tamen ex omnibus praemiis uirtutis, si esset habenda ratio praemiorum, amplissimum esse praemium gloriam; esse hanc unam, quae breuitatem uitae posteritatis memoria consolaretur, quae efficeret ut absentes adessemus, mortui uiueremus.' Cf. *Mil.* 72.

14. *Mil.* 2, 15, 70.

15. *Mil.* 3.

16. *Mil.* 21.

17. Stone (1980); Berry (1993).

18. *Mil.* 65: 'laudabam equidem incredibilem diligentiam Cn. Pompei, sed dicam, ut sentio, iudices. nimis multa audire coguntur neque aliter facere possunt ei, quibus commissa tota res publica est.'

19. *Mil.* 73, 78-9, 87-8.

20. *Mil.* 65-6, Asc. *Mil.* 36-8.

21. Asc. *Mil.* 35.

22. Asc. *Mil.* 36.

23. *Mil.* 69, 80, 93-8.

24. *Mil.* 68: 'probasset ... tribunatum suum ad salutem meam, quae tibi carissima fuisset, consiliis tuis gubernatum; ....'

25. *Mil.* 65.

26. *Mil.* 105: 'sed finis sit; neque enim prae lacrimis iam loqui possumus, et hic se lacrimis defendi uetat.'

27. But cf. Quint. *Inst.* 11.3.173, who praises this sentence's effectiveness as an indication of the speaker's exhaustion. Is it significant that he does not consider the final words?

28. *Mil.* 105: 'uos oro obtestorque, iudices, ut in sententiis ferendis, quod sentietis, id audeatis. uestram uirtutem, iustitiam, fidem, mihi credite, is maxime comprobabit, qui in iudicibus legendis optimum et sapientissimum et fortissimum quemque elegit.'

29. Dio 40.54.3.

30. Douglas (1973); Wisse (1995).

31. *Orat.* 1: 'utrum difficilius aut maius esset negare tibi saepius idem roganti an efficere id quod rogares diu multumque, Brute, dubitaui.'

32. *Orat.* 2: 'quid enim est maius quam, cum tanta sit inter oratores bonos dissimilitudo, iudicare quae sit optima species et quasi figura dicendi?'

33. *Orat.* 7: 'atque ego in summo oratore fingendo talem informabo qualis fortasse nemo fuit.'

34. Individual: 100, 237; speech, 52, 112.

35. *Fam.* 7.33; 9.16.7; 9.18; Rawson (1983) 213-16.

36. *Or.* 43: 'nulla praecepta ponemus'; 51: 'atque in primis duabus dicendi partibus qualis esset summatim breuiterque descripsimus'; 55: 'de

quo plura dicerem, si hoc praecipiendi tempus esset aut si tuo hoc quaereres'; 73: 'magnus est locus hic, Brute, quod te non fugit, et magnum uolumen aliud desiderat; sed ad id quod agitur illud satis'; 87: 'utetur utroque; sed altero in narrando aliquid uenuste, altero in iaciendo mittendoque ridiculo, cuius genera plura sunt; sed nunc aliud agimus.'

37. *Or.* 22: 'atque utinam in Latinis talis oratoris simulacrum reperire possemus! esset egregrium non quaerere externa, domesticis esse contentos.'

38. *Or.* 102-3, 107-12, 210-11, 223-6, 232-3. See Narducci (2002: 439-42).

39. *Or.* 103: 'quae exempla selegissem, nisi uel nota esse arbitrarer uel ipsi possent legere qui quaererent.'

40. *Or.* 108: 'nemo enim orator tam multa ne in Graeco quidem otio scripsit quam multa sunt nostra, eaque hanc ipsam habent quam probo uarietatem.'

41. Yon (1964) 122-67.

42. *Att.* 12.40; *Att.* 13.37, 48; *Fam.* 9.12.

43. It is not clear to me that *Att.* 13.48.2 does imply that Porcia had been dead some time: Cicero's vague recollection could as much be the result of a recent but cursory skim as of a reading in the remoter past. But it remains the case that he *elected* to write on this subject.

44. *Att.* 12.38a.1; 12.40.2-3.

45. Bringmann (1971).

46. *Div.* 2.1: 'quaerenti mihi multumque et diu cogitanti quanam re possem prodesse quam plurimis, ne quando intermitterem consulere rei publicae, nulla maior occurrebat quam si optimarum artium uias traderem mei ciuibus; quod compluribus iam libris me arbitror consecutum.'

47. Cf. Schofield (2002). Unless one wishes to posit book by book dissemination for Cicero's philosophical work, he could presumably have added a reference to Caesar's death at the beginning of the first book of *Div*.

48. *Att.* 16.6.4.

49. Books 1-2 are set in 50, on the eve of the civil war, and Cicero's interlocutors Torquatus and Triarius both died during the civil war. (They are paired already in *Brut.* 265-6, though whether this is due to particularly close friendship, similarity of age, deaths at the same point in the conflict, or other factors, is unclear.) Books 3-4 involve the younger Cato, whose death at Utica was already linked symbolically with the death of freedom.

50. As is Nigidius Figulus, conversation with whom (and Cratippus, who was still alive) seems to have been presented as the stimulus to Cicero's version of Plato's *Timaeus*: indeed, the preface acts as a very brief obituary of Nigidius.

51. *Stoic paradoxes, On ends, On the nature of the gods, Tusculan disputations*.

52. Steel (2003).

160

53. One can note too the dedication in the summer of 44 of the *Topica* to Trebatius.

54. *ad Brut.* 2.3.4. On the background to *Philippics*, see Frisch (1946); Shackleton Bailey (1986).

55. *ad Att.* 15.13.1.

56. Cicero uses the familiar technique of remarking upon his opponent's demeanour to add verisimilitude: *Phil.* 2.36, 2.76, in addition to frequent second person apostrophes and a reference to the possibility of a reply (2.111).

57. Cf. 1.27.; Hall (2002) 274-5.

58. *Phil.* 2.57.

59. *Phil.* 1.8: 'Antonium, repudiatis malis suasoribus, remissis prouinciis Galliis, ad auctoritatem senatus esse rediturum.'

60. *Phil.* 1.34: 'libertate esse parem ceteris, principem dignitate.'

61. *Phil.* 2.11: 'qui consulatus uerbo meus, patres conscripti, re uester fuit. quid enim ego constitui, quid gessi, quid egi nisi ex huius ordinis consilio, auctoritate, sententia?'

62. *Phil.* 2.108.

63. *Phil.* 1.28; 2.118.

64. *Phil.* 2.12-14.

65. See Shackleton Bailey (1979) 280-5.

66. *Phil.* 8.1-4.

67. The *Catilinarian* crisis developed over some months: but Cicero's difficulty, in that case, seems not to have been the existence of a clearly-defined and identifiable opposition, but rather that many people did not believe that the threat existed. And Cicero was not present in Rome as the stand-off between Pompeius and Caesar developed in 50.

68. *ad Brut.* 2.4.2.

69. Caesar's works remain astonishingly understudied, but see Welch and Powell (1998).

70. Rawson (1985) provides an exhaustive account of what was going on in the late Republic.

Chronological Appendix of Cicero's Works other than his Letters

Speeches are listed under the year they were delivered. Speeches which appear never to have been disseminated in written form are not included. All dates are BC.

Before 81	*On invention* (*de inuentione*)
	Pontius Glaucus
	Phaenomena (translation of Aratus' poem)
	Nilus
	Vxorius
	Alcyones
81	*On behalf of Quinctius* (*pro Quinctio*)
80	*On behalf of Roscius from Ameria* (*pro Roscio Amerino*)
75	*As quaestor when leaving Lilybaeum* (*cum quaestor Lilybaeo decederet*)
71	*On behalf of Tullius* (*pro Tullio*)
70	*Against Caecilius at the preliminary hearing* (*diuinatio in Caecilium*)
	First hearing against Verres (*in Verrem actio prima*)
	Second hearing against Verres (*in Verrem actio secunda*)
69	*On behalf of Fonteius* (*pro Fonteio*)
	On behalf of Caecina (*pro Caecina*)
67	*On behalf of Oppius* (*pro Oppio*)
66	*On the command of Gnaeus Pompeius* (*de imperio Cn. Pompei*)
	On behalf of Cluentius (*pro Cluentio*)
	On behalf of Gaius Manilius (*pro C. Manilio*)
65	*On behalf of Cornelius* (*pro Cornelio*)
	On the Alexandrian king (*de rege Alexandrino*)
64	*Whilst a candidate* (*in toga candida*)
	On behalf of Gallius (*pro Gallio*)

63	*On the agrarian law I-III (de lege agraria I-III)*
	On Otho (de Othone)
	On behalf of Gaius Rabirius accused of high treason (pro C. Rabirio perduellionis reo)
	On the sons of the proscribed (de proscriptorum filiis)
	Against Catiline I-IV (in Catilinam I-IV)
	On behalf of Murena (pro Murena)
	When I gave up my province at a contio (cum prouinciam in contione deposui)
62	*Against Quintus Metellus' public meeting (contra contionem Q. Metelli)*
	On behalf of Archias (pro Archia)
	On behalf of Sulla (pro Sulla)
61	*Against Clodius and Curio (in Clodium et Curionem)*
60	*His consulship (Consulatus suus)*
59	*On behalf of Flaccus (pro Flacco)*
57	*After his return to the Senate (post reditum in Senatu)*
	After his return to the people (post reditum ad Quirites)
	On his house (de domo sua)
56	*On behalf of Sestius (pro Sestio)*
	Against Vatinius (in Vatinium)
	On the soothsayers' answers (de haruspicum responsis)
	On behalf of Caelius (pro Caelio)
	On behalf of Lucius Cornelius Balbus (pro Balbo)
	Concerning the consular provinces (de prouinciis consularibus)
55	*Against Lucius Piso (in Pisonem)*
	On the orator (de oratore)
54	*On behalf of Scaurus (pro Scauro)*
	On behalf of Plancius (pro Plancio)
	On behalf of Rabirius Postumus (pro Rabirio Postumo)
	On his vicissitudes (de temporibus suis)
53	*On Milo's debts (de aere alieno Milonis)*
52	*On behalf of Milo (pro Milone)*
	On the state (de republica)
51	*On the laws (de legibus)*
46	*Brutus (Brutus)*
	Paradoxes of the Stoics (Paradoxa Stoicorum)
	Cato (Cato)
	On the best kind of orator (de optimo genere oratorum)
	Orator (Orator)
	On behalf of Marcellus (pro Marcello)
	On behalf of Ligarius (pro Ligario)
	The divisions of oratory (Partitiones oratoriae)
45	*Consolation (Consolatio)*

	Hortensius (Hortensius)
	Academica (Academica)
	On ends (de finibus)
	Tusculan disputations (Tusculanae disputationes)
	On behalf of King Deiotarus (pro rege Deiotaro)
	Praise of Porcia (Laudatio Porciae)
	Timaeus (Timaeus)
44	*On the nature of the Gods (de natura deorum)*
	On divination (de diuinatione)
	On fate (de fato)
	Cato on old age (Cato de senectute)
	On glory (de gloria)
	Laelius on friendship (Laelius de amicitia)
	Topics (Topica)
	On duties (de officiis)
	Philippics I-IV (Philippicae I-IV)
43	*Philippics V-XIV (Philippicae V-XIV)*
	Against Publius Servilius Isauricus (in P. Seruilium Isauricum)
Of uncertain date	*On behalf of Fundanius (pro Fundanio)*
	On behalf of Roscius the actor (pro Roscio Comoedo)
	On behalf of Varenus (pro Vareno)
	Marius (Marius)
	Oeconomicus (Oeconomicus)

Bibliography

Alexander, M.C. (1990), *Trials in the Late Roman Republic, 149 BC to 50 BC* (Toronto: University of Toronto Press).

Axer, J. (1979). *The Style and the Composition of Cicero's Speech 'Pro Q. Roscio Comoedo': Origin and Function* (Warsaw: Wydawnictwa Uniwersytetu Warszawskiego).

Beard, M. (2002), 'Ciceronian correspondences: making a book out of letters', in *Classics in Progress: essays on ancient Greece and Rome*, ed. T.P. Wiseman (Oxford: OUP), 103-44.

Beard, M. and Crawford, M. (1999). *Rome in the Late Republic: problems and interpretations* (London: Duckworth).

Berry, D.H. (1993). 'Pompey's legal knowledge – or lack of it: Cic. *Mil.* 70 and the date of *Pro Milone*', *Historia* 42: 502-4.

Berry, D.H. (1996). *Cicero pro Sulla Oratio* (Cambridge: CUP).

Berry, D.H. (2000). *Cicero: Defence Speeches* (Oxford: OUP).

Bringmann, K. (1971). *Untersuchungen zum spaten Cicero* (Gottingen: Vandenhoeck & Ruprecht).

Bringmann, K. (1986). 'Der Diktator Caesar als Richter? Zu Ciceros Reden "Pro Ligario" und "Pro Rege Deiotaro".' *Hermes* 141: 72-88.

Brittain, C. (2001). *Philo of Larissa: the last of the academic sceptics* (Oxford: OUP).

Brunt, P.A. (1988). *The Fall of the Roman Republic* (Oxford: OUP).

Butler, S. (2002). *The Hand of Cicero* (London: Routledge).

Classen, C.J. (1985). *Recht, Rhetorik, Politik: Untersuchungen zu Ciceros rhetorischer Strategie* (Darmstadt: Wissenschaftliche Buchgesellschaft).

Corbeill, A. (2002). 'Rhetorical education in Cicero's youth', in *Brill's Companion to Cicero: oratory and rhetoric*, ed. J.M. May (Leiden: Brill), 23-48.

Cotton, H.M. (1986). 'The role of Cicero's letters of recommendation: Iustitia versus gratia?', *Hermes* 114: 443-60.

Courtney, E. (1993). *The Fragmentary Latin Poets* (Oxford: OUP).

Craig, C.P. (1993), *Form as Argument in Cicero's Speeches: a study of dilemma* (Atlanta: Scholars Press).

Craig, C.P. (2002). 'Selected recent work on rhetorica and speeches', in

Brill's Companion to Cicero: rhetoric and oratory, ed. J.M. May (Leiden: Brill).

Crawford, J.W. (1984), *Cicero: the lost and unpublished orations* (Gottingen: Vandenhoeck and Ruprecht).

Crawford, J.W. (1994). *M. Tullius Cicero, the fragmentary speeches: an edition with commentary* (Atlanta: Scholars Press).

Crawford, J.W. (2002). 'The lost and fragmentary orations', in *Brill's Companion to Cicero: rhetoric and oratory*, ed. J.M. May (Leiden: Brill).

Crawford, M. (1978). *The Roman Republic* (London: Fontana).

Cugusi, P. (1970). *Epistolographi minores Latini* (Turin: Paravia).

Cugusi, P. (1983). *Evoluzione e forme dell' epistolografia Latina* (Rome: Herder).

Douglas, A.E. (1968). *Cicero* (Oxford: OUP).

Douglas, A.E. (1973). 'The intellectual background of Cicero's rhetorica: a study in method', *ANRW* 1.3: 95-138.

Drummond, A. (1995). *Law, Power, Politics: Sallust and the execution of the Catilinarian conspirators* (Stuttgart: Franz Steiner).

Flower, H. (1996). *Ancestor Masks and Aristocratic Culture in Roman culture* (Oxford: OUP).

Frisch, H. (1946). *Cicero's Fight for the Republic: the historical background of Cicero's Philippics* (Copenhagen: Gyldendal).

Gelzer, M. (1969). *The Roman Nobility* (Oxford: Blackwell).

Goar, R.J. (1987). *The Legend of Cato Uticensis from the First Century* BC *to the Fifth Century* AD (Brussels: Latomus).

Goldberg, S.M. (1995). *Epic in Republican Rome* (New York: Oxford University Press).

Goodwin, J. (2001). 'Cicero's authority', *Philosophy and Rhetoric* 34.1: 38-60.

Görler, W. (1988). 'From Athens to Tusculum: gleaning the background of Cicero's *de oratore*', *Rhetorica* 6.3: 215-35.

Gotoff, H.C. (1993). *Cicero's Caesarian Speeches: a stylistic commentary* (Chapel Hill: University of North Carolina Press).

Gowers, E. (1993). *The Loaded Table: representations of food in Roman literature* (Oxford: OUP).

Griffin, M.T. (1997). 'The composition of the *Academica*: motives and versions', in *Assent and Argument: studies in Cicero's Academic books*, ed. B. Inwood and J. Mansfeld (Leiden: Brill), 1-35.

Gruen, E.S. (1971). *The Last Generation of the Roman Republic* (Berkeley: University of California Press).

Gruen, E.S. (1990). *Studies in Greek Culture and Roman Policy* (Leiden: Brill).

Gruen, E.S. (1992). *Culture and National Identity in Republican Rome* (Ithaca: Cornell University Press).

Habinek, T. and Schiesaro, A., ed. (1997). *The Roman Cultural Revolution* (Cambridge: CUP).

Bibliography

Hall, J. (1994). 'Persuasive design in Cicero's *De oratore*', *Phoenix* 48: 210-25.

Hall, J. (2002). 'The *Philippics*', in *Brill's Companion to Cicero: oratory and rhetoric*, ed. J.M. May (Leiden: Brill).

Harrison, S.J. (1990). 'Cicero's "de temporibus suis": the evidence reconsidered', *Hermes* 118: 455-63.

Hellegouarc'h, J. (1963). *Le vocabulaire Latin des relations et des partis politique sous la Republique* (Paris: Les Belles Lettres).

Humbert, J. (1925). *Les plaidoyers ecrits et les plaidoiries réelles de Ciceron* (Paris: Presses Universitaires de France).

Hutchinson, G.O. (1998). *Cicero's Correspondence: a literary study* (Oxford: OUP).

Kennedy, G.A. (1994). *A New History of Classical Rhetoric* (Princeton: Princeton University Press).

Kenney, E.J. (1982). 'Books and readers in the Roman world', in *The Cambridge History of Classical Literature: the early Republic*, ed. E.J. Kenney (Cambridge: Cambridge University Press).

Kinsey, T.E. (1971). *M. Tullii Ciceronis pro P. Quinctio oratio* (Sydney: Sydney University Press).

Krostenko, B. (2001). *Cicero, Catullus and the Language of Social Performance* (Chicago: University of Chicago Press).

Krumeich, R., Pechstein, N., Seidensticker, B. (1999). *Das griechische Satyrspiel* (Darmstadt: Wissenschaftliche Buchgesellschaft).

Laurence, R. and Berry, J., ed. (1998). *Cultural Identity in the Roman Empire* (London: Routledge).

Leeman, A.D., Pinkster, H. et al. (1981-). *M. Tullius Cicero de oratore libri III. Kommentar* (Heidelberg: Carl Winter).

Lenaghan, J.O. (1969). *A Commentary on Cicero's Oration De Haruspicum Responsis* (The Hague: Mouton).

Lightfoot, J.L. (1999). *Parthenius of Nicaea* (Oxford: OUP).

Lintott, A.W. (1999). *The Constitution of the Roman Republic* (Oxford: OUP).

Marshall, B.A. (1987). '*Excepta oratio*, the other *Pro Milone* and the question of shorthand', *Latomus* 46: 730-6.

May, J.M. (1988). *Trials of Character: the eloquence of Ciceronian ethos* (Chapel Hill: University of North Carolina Press).

May, J.M. and Wisse, J. (2001). *Cicero: On the Ideal Orator* (New York: OUP).

May, J.M., ed. (2002). *Brill's Companion to Cicero: oratory and rhetoric* (Leiden: Brill).

McDermott, W. (1972). 'Cicero's publication of his consular speeches', *Philologus* 116: 277-84.

Meier, C. (1962). 'Pompeius' Rückkehr aus dem Mithridatischen Kriege und die Catilinarische Verschwörung', *Athenaeum* 40: 103-25.

Mitchell, T.N. (1979). *Cicero: the ascending years* (New Haven: Yale UP).

Mitchell, T.N. (1991). *Cicero: the senior statesman* (New Haven, Yale UP).

Narducci, E. (2002). 'Orator and the definition of the ideal orator', in *Brill's Companion to Cicero: oratory and rhetoric*, ed. J.M. May (Leiden: Brill).

Nicholson, J. (1994). 'The delivery and confidentiality of Cicero's letters', *Classical Journal* 90.1: 33-63.

Powell, J.G.F. (1990). *Cicero: On Friendship and The Dream of Scipio* (Warminster: Aris and Phillips).

Powell, J.G.F. (1994). 'The *rector rei publicae* of Cicero's *De Republica*', *Scripta Classica Israelica* 13: 19-29.

Rawson, E. (1971). 'Lucius Crassus and Cicero: the formation of a statesman', *Proceedings of the Cambridge Philological Society* 17: 75-88.

Rawson, E. (1983). *Cicero: a portrait* (London: Bristol Classical Press).

Rawson, E. (1985). *Intellectual Life in the Late Roman Republic* (London: Duckworth).

Riggsby, A.M. (1995). 'Pliny on Cicero and oratory: self-fashioning in the public eye', *American Journal of Philology* 116: 123-35.

Schmidt, P.L. (2001). 'The original version of the *De Re Publica* and the *De Legibus*', in *Cicero's Republic*, ed. J.G.F. Powell and J.A. North (London: Institute of Classical Studies).

Schneider, W.C. (1998). *Vom Handeln der Römer* (Hildesheim: Georg Olms).

Schofield, M. (2002). 'Academic therapy: Philo of Larissa and Cicero's project in the *Tusculans*', in *Philosophy and Power in the Graeco-Roman World*, ed. G. Clark and T. Rajak (Oxford: OUP).

Seager, R. (1979). *Pompey: a political biography* (Oxford: Blackwell).

Settle, J.N. (1963). 'The trial of Milo and the other *Pro Milone*', *TAPhA* 94: 268-80.

Shackleton Bailey, D.R. (1965). *Cicero's Letters to Atticus,* vol. 1 (Cambridge: CUP).

Shackleton Bailey, D.R. (1977). *Cicero: Epistulae ad Familiares* (Cambridge: CUP).

Shackleton Bailey, D.R. (1979). 'On Cicero's speeches', *Harvard Studies in Classical Philology* 83: 238-85.

Shackleton Bailey, D.R. (1986). *Philippicae* (Chapel Hill: University of North Carolina Press).

Shackleton Bailey, D.R. (1988). *M. Tullius Ciceronis Epistulae ad Quintum fratrem, epistulae ad M. Brutum; accedunt commentariolum petitionis, fragementa epistularum* (Stuttgart: Teubner).

Sharples, R.W. (1986). 'Cicero's *Republic* and Greek political theory', *Polis* 5.2: 30-50.

Spielvogel, J. (1993). *Amicitia und res publica* (Stuttgart: F. Steiner).

Starr, R.J. (1987). 'The circulation of literary texts in the Roman world', *Classical Quarterly* 37.1: 213-23.

Steel, C.E.W. (2001). *Cicero, Rhetoric, and Empire* (Oxford: OUP).

Bibliography

Steel, C.E.W. (2003). 'Cicero's *Brutus*: the end of oratory and the beginning of history?', *Bulletin of the Institute of Classical Studies* 46:195-211.

Stockton, D. (1971). *Cicero: a political biography* (Oxford: OUP).

Stone, A.M. (1980). '*Pro Milone*: Cicero's second thoughts' *Antichthon* 14: 88-111.

Stroh, W. (1975). *Taxis und Taktik: die advokatische Dispositionskunst in Ciceros Gerichtsreden* (Stuttgart: Teubner).

Tatum, W.J. (1999). *P. Clodius Pulcher: the patrician tribune* (Chapel Hill: University of North Carolina Press).

Vasaly, A. (1993). *Representation: Images of the World in Ciceronian Oratory* (Berkeley: University of California Press).

Vickers, B. (1988). *In Defence of Rhetoric* (Oxford: Oxford University Press).

Welch, K. and Powell, A., ed. (1998). *Julius Caesar as Artful Reporter* (London: Duckworth with The Classical Press of Wales).

White, P. (2003). 'Tactics in Caesar's correspondence with Cicero', *Proceedings of the Langford Latin Seminar* 11: 68-95.

Wiseman, T.P. (1998). 'The publication of *De Bello Gallico*', in *Julius Caesar as Artful Reporter*, ed. K. Welch and A. Powell (London: Duckworth with The Classical Press of Wales), 1-9.

Wisse, J. (1989). *Ethos and Pathos: from Aristotle to Cicero* (Amsterdam: Hakkert).

Wisse, J. (1995). 'Greeks, Romans, and the rise of Atticism', in *Greek Literary Theory After Aristotle: a collection of papers in honour of D.M. Schenkeveld*, ed. J.G.J. Abbenes, S.R. Slings and I. Sluiter (Amsterdam, VU University Press), 65-82.

Wooten, C.W. (1983). *Cicero's Philippics and their Demosthenic Model* (Chapel Hill: University of North Carolina Press).

Yon, A. (1964). *Cicéron l'orateur* (Paris: Les Belles Lettres)

Zetzel, J.E.G. (1995). *Cicero: de re publica* (Cambridge: CUP).

Zetzel, J.E.G. (1972). 'Cicero and the Scipionic circle', *Harvard Studies in Classical Philology* 76: 173-9.

Index

Index

174

Index